When We Hear From God –

A Collection of True Stories of Ordinary People

By Holly Placencia and Jill Kidd

TABLE OF CONTENTS

Table of Contents (Continued)

Table of Contents (Continued)

FORWARD

I've been told I'm a good listener. Whether that is true or not I'm not sure, but I do know I don't always listen to the voice of the Lord as well as I should. Maybe you can relate. There are so many times it would be best to quiet myself and listen. Yet how difficult that can be with so much "noise" in the world coming at us from every direction.

With that thought in mind, you hold in your hands a very precious gift. The gift of the challenge and encouragement to listen. And not just to anyone, but to listen to the "Word made flesh," to Christ Himself, and to the Holy Spirit. Isn't it amazing that the One who spoke you and I into existence is still speaking today? Are we listening?

As you read this book, you will find yourself blessed time and time again by the true stories of ordinary people, just like yourself, who stopped long enough to hear the Lord saying words to them. Words of faith. Words of hope. Words of healing. Also in the following pages are poems and personal journal entries that will inspire you to lean in closer to God to hear the life-giving words He has to say to you. Words of comfort. Words of joy. Words of love.

I have known the authors of this book for about four years, and I have to say I couldn't think of two people more qualified to write and compile a book on hearing the voice of God. These are women of God who shine the light of Christ because they have stopped often enough to hear God speak. Their character and their lives prove that God still speaks today to those who will stop and listen. They speak from experience. They have walked through deep waters and have learned some things about listening to the voice of their Lord. And the others who share their story in this book share from first-hand experience.

I believe you will be blessed by this unique and God-inspired book. As you read, I encourage you to stop from time to time and say, "God, what are You saying to me?" Then listen and be amazed by what happens "When We Hear From God!"

Greg Boatright, Lead Pastor
Church on the Hill, Redlands, California

DEDICATIONS

Holly would like to dedicate this book to her husband:

John Placencia

And to her six sons, the Livingston boys:

Joseph
Benjamin
Thomas
David
Daniel
Jonathan

And to her grandson, Logan
And to her daughter-in-law, Mackenzie

******

Jill would like to dedicate this book to her family:

Greg, Jo Ann, Noah & Hannah Hernandez
Brian, Kovie & Kaylee Kidd

About the Authors

Holly Placencia is a 55 year-old woman married to John Placencia. Between the two of them, they have eight children and three grandchildren. She works as a special education teacher for the severely disabled. She has taught special education for seven years. Before that, she was a preschool teacher for eight years. She has a master's degree and credentials in both mild/moderate and moderate/severe special education. Holly has spent many years teaching Sunday school and, a portion of that time, leading the children's ministry at church.

Jill Kidd is a 70 year-old woman, mother of two and grandmother of four. She worked as a secretary for over 40 years in many fields including construction, real estate, law, science, and education. She taught adult school secretarial courses, and later received a ministerial license through U.E.C. She has been a Sunday school teacher, youth director, women's leader, church board member, church secretary/treasurer, and assistant pastor.

Introduction
by Holly

Does God speak to people today? Can we hear His voice? Does He have more than a 3-word vocabulary? The answers to these questions are yes, yes, and a resounding YES!

Most of my life, I have heard that God answers prayers with just three words-- "yes," "no," or "wait." But I have found out over the years that God answers prayers in a multiple of different ways! You will discover after reading this collection of testimonials that God is very creative in how He answers prayers and how He speaks to His children. He will give the exact words a person needs at the exact time they need it. He is a loving God who truly cares about His children. Sometimes He gives a word of encouragement, or a rebuke, or a word of knowledge, or a word of direction. Many times He speaks to His children directly from the Word of God, or through other people, or by a quickening of the spirit. Some people have heard the audible voice of God; others have had dreams or visions. Some believe God has used angels to speak to them.

God is always speaking. He speaks every language in the world and His vocabulary exceeds the most brilliant linguist! He knows every individual heart and what our deepest needs are. In fact, He knows our needs far better than we know ourselves! He hears our prayers and He answers them. When I cried out to Him during a stressful time of my life, He didn't remove me from the difficult situation. He didn't tell me "no" or "wait." He told me that His presence would go with me and that's how I would find rest. Those were the words I needed to hear at that time! God loves His children and desires to have fellowship with us. He doesn't want any of us to fall away and will gladly lead each one in the right path. That's why He gave us the Holy Spirit, so He can guide us into all truth.

But do you have the Holy Spirit? Have you been born again? The first step to hearing God's voice is to receive Jesus Christ as your personal Savior. Pray to God and admit that you are a sinner. Confess your sins to Him and ask Him to forgive you. Then receive God's gift of eternal life by believing on His son, Jesus Christ. When you receive Christ into your life, you are ready to have a personal and intimate relationship with the living God! You are ready to listen and hear His voice.

He is so ready to speak to us. The question is, are we listening? There are so many distractions in our world today. It's not always easy to hear the voice of God. We have to quiet ourselves before God and block out the distractions so we can hear Him. Then we have to be willing to obey, too. In the Bible, God stopped talking to King Saul because he wasn't interested in actually obeying God (I Samuel 28:6). But when our hearts are open before Him and ready to receive, He will begin to speak to us.

Do you want to hear God's voice? Pray, and ask Him to speak to you. Sit quietly before Him. Listen to the Holy Spirit inside of you. Read the Bible and meditate on scriptures. Open your heart before the Lord and receive whatever He has for you. Surrender your will to His. Seek the Lord and you will find Him.

"You will seek Me and find Me when you seek Me with all your heart."

Jeremiah 29:13 (NIV)

*Your own ears will hear Him.
Right behind you a voice will say,
"This is the way you should go,"
whether to the right or to the left.*

Isaiah 30:21 (NLT)

Holly's Story

I was born in Ohio on Christmas Day, 1963. But I only lived there for six years until my parents decided to become missionaries. So in 1970, my mom, dad, sister, brother, and I packed up and went to the mission field for the next 10 years. First we lived in Ecuador, then we moved to Papua New Guinea, where my mom and dad had two more little girls. My dad was a missionary pilot. He led me to the Lord when I was seven years old. He taught me the importance of reading the Bible, going to church, and loving other people. My parents were devout Christians, but far from perfect. I wish I could say that from the time I became a Christian I made all the right decisions, but that just isn't the truth. My life has been a journey of many ups and downs.

When I was 16, we settled down in California, where I have lived ever since. Soon after high school, I got married and started having kids right away. I ended up having six boys! I loved having kids, but I had no clue how to be a wife. I had no clue how to pick a husband in the first place! He and I were worlds apart. I was wrapped up in my kids and he was out doing his own thing.

After 13 years of marriage, I found myself divorced and raising six little boys on my own. I had no career since I had always been a stay-at-home mom. But I knew I had to do something. So I went back to school and earned a degree in special education. I often worried about my children, since I was so busy and their father was very unstable and inconsistent in their lives. But one day as I was praying, I felt God speak to my heart. He told me not to worry about my children because He was their Father and He would take care of them. This brought me peace and comfort, knowing God was their Heavenly Father and He had everything under control.

As time went on, I had other encounters with the Lord, where I knew He had spoken directly to my heart. Many times it was through a passage in the Bible that jumped out at me at just the right time. Sometimes it was through another person, or just a quickening in my own spirit. One day a co-worker gave me a devotional book as a Christmas gift. It was full of passages where the author felt God speak to her directly, and she shared those passages with the world. But the part that really spoke to me was in the forward. She mentioned how she would go to quiet places and just listen to God, then write down what God would speak to her heart. When I read that, I thought, "If she can do that, then I can too." So that began my journey of "listening to God." I started listening, and I filled up journals with what God had spoken to my heart. You will find samples of those scattered throughout this book.

This book began with a desire to share with others that God is speaking today. He is speaking to you and to me and to all who desire to hear His voice. But the only way we can hear Him is if we stop, and listen to His voice. I know that many Christians around the world have heard the voice of God and have a story to tell. Some have heard the audible voice of God, but most of the time He is heard through a quickening in their spirit. It's something they feel inside and they know that they know it was God speaking to them. This book is a compilation of those stories. I hope you are blessed and inspired as you read each one.

Listen To Me
Inspiration received by Holly Placencia

I am everything you need. I am here and I am talking to you. It's no big mystery. Just listen and write. I'm not so far that I can't be heard. I desire relationships with My people. I am close by. Don't think I can only be heard at times or in very mysterious ways. As it says, "The Word of God is near you, even in your mouth." Go and speak. You have the Word of God in you. Go and speak it. Then you will find joy.

But as it is written:
"Eye has not seen, nor ear heard,
nor have entered into the heart of man
the things which God has prepared
for those who love Him."
But God has revealed them to us
through His Spirit.
For the Spirit searches all things,
yes, the deep things of God.

I Corinthians 2:9-10 (NKJV)

Jill's Story

I was raised in church; my family attended faithfully every Sunday. I considered myself to be a Christian. I think everyone did back then, at least in the midwest where I grew up. I came from a military family so we moved a lot. It was just after my 16th birthday that my family moved from Michigan to Southern California. What a culture shock for all of us! It took quite a bit of adjustment, but soon I was able to make new friends and enjoy this new beginning.

At 18, I graduated from high school and started attending the junior college in town. That's when a cute sailor boy I knew returned from his second tour of duty in Vietnam and looked me up. By December, he had received orders to the East Coast. I left college to marry him and we were off to Charleston, S.C. Another culture shock for this midwestern girl!

Then, at age 27, my whole world crumbled. My marriage ended! Heartbroken, I packed up our two children, ages 7 and 4, and headed home to Southern California. It was a very difficult time in my life but I tried to hold it all together for the sake of my children and my parents. My faith was wavering and it seemed like I no longer had the answers I once thought I had.

I began a search for spiritual truth. Unfortunately, I went down many wrong roads which only confused me more. Around this time, I attended a new-age training that seemed to be so enlightening. I thought I had finally found what I was looking for! While I was still on a euphoric high, brainwashed into believing I had control over my universe, I met and married my second husband. I was 32 years old; my kids were 12 and 9, and he had a son who was 10. We began a blended family and I was convinced life could be good again.

Less than a year into the marriage, I realized I had made a big mistake. But I took my marriage vows seriously and tried to make the best of it. So I suggested we get back into church. I was raised Methodist; he was raised Baptist. I wanted to find a Methodist church; he insisted we find a Baptist church. I had heard a little about those Baptists and I didn't want to go there!

As it turned out, it was the best thing that ever happened to me and my children. I heard for the first time that we must be born again. They told us that we are saved by grace and not by works. I found out that I could have a personal relationship with the Living God! The Holy Spirit began to introduce Himself to me in a very intimate way. The pastor had an altar call at the end of the sermon and told us, "God loves you just the way you are, but He loves you too much to leave you that way!" I accepted Jesus Christ as my personal Lord and Savior that day in May 1981. So did all three of our children!

That evening when I got home, I was alone with my thoughts. I was thinking about all that had happened that day and, in my mind, I questioned the idea of giving Jesus control of my life. At that time in my life, it seemed like I had just regained control after all that had happened since my divorce. I was uneasy about giving up what control I felt I had finally achieved. Suddenly I heard a voice in the room. He said:

> **"You can have control anytime you want it,**
> **but *you* don't know where you're going."**

I instantly envisioned myself running hard in a maze, like a mouse, and getting nowhere! I sat up and looked around to see who was speaking. It was a definite voice I heard! But there was no one in the room but me. That's the first time I really heard His voice, and I never forgot it! He continues to guide me and I am so thankful for that. By myself, I kept getting off track. Something wonderful happened when I surrendered my life to Jesus. He gave me stability and, even though my circumstances were the same, *I* was different. No longer could I be so easily misled. No longer was I tossed about by every wind that blew. I was grounded in the Truth, and He continues to shed light upon my path.

As time went on, I began writing poems. It was really a most amazing thing – I would begin to take a nap, and suddenly the words of a poem would so overwhelm me that I would have to get up and start writing. It often happened in the night as well, so I began keeping a pad of paper and a pen next to my bed. I couldn't go back to sleep until it was written down. It never took long. It seemed to me that the words were flowing from the heart of God Himself, and it was a very personal thing between the Lord and me. It wasn't until several years later that I realized these poems are a record of my own spiritual journey. I still get choked up when I read them, and am instantly in remembrance of the event that had occurred in my personal life that prompted each poem. I have enclosed many of them between the pages of this book. I believe each to be inspired by the Lord and hope you sense His presence, as I did, in each poem.

JUST ME

None of us is perfect; and least of all, me;
I just report through poetry what God gives for me to see.
Will you take my hand and walk with me through journeys yet untold?
For, together, we will truly see God's promises unfold.

Look Up!

When the world has given up,
And the dark has settled in,
And the crushing sound of silence fills our ears -
Look Up!

When there's nowhere else to go
And nothing else to try,
And the courage that was ours just disappears -
Look Up!

When our lonely hearts are breaking,
And there's nothing left worth taking,
And the beauty all around us has all gone -
Look Up!

When we hear the children crying,
But we know we are alone
And the cries that we are hearing are our own -
Look Up!

Look up; look up; for your redemption draweth nigh.
It is God who has been waiting all this time.
While we were running through the mazes, causing havoc with our lives,
God was waiting 'til the day we would look up!

Jill Kidd

You said,
"Listen and I will speak!"

Job 42:4 (NLT)

Called
by Holly

I grew up as a missionary kid in the 1970's. We lived off the support of several American churches, so it was necessary for my parents to go from church to church explaining what they were doing. They would show slides of the mission field, and they would always tell the story of how they were called to be missionaries. As a child, I heard this story many times. My mom and dad would each take their turn in telling the different parts, and I always listened with anticipation, knowing exactly what part was coming next. It's been over 40 years since I've heard them tell this story, but it was so ingrained in my mind that I'm fairly confident I can retell it now. (I'll have my mom check it later for accuracy).

My parents lived in Ohio and had three little kids (my older sister, me, and my younger brother). They had just bought a house, and my dad had a good job flying for Goodyear Tires. My mom stayed busy caring for us kids full-time. In her spare time, and as her way of relaxing, she played the piano. My mom loved her piano! Several times on any given day, she would sit down and fill the house with beautiful music! Or sometimes it was funny music that we would all dance to! This was just who my mom was, and still is today.

Life was good for my family. We attended a church called, "The Chapel on Fir Hill." My dad also attended a men's group associated with the Mennonites. Occasionally, missionaries would come to this group and tell their stories. They told of their need for financial support and also the need for more missionaries on the field. My dad was very interested and willingly gave financial donations. Of course, the other part didn't apply to him at all. There was no way he could actually become a missionary. My dad was no preacher! And he was definitely no Bible translator! He had never even been to college.

But one day after enjoying a men's fellowship breakfast, he had a conversation with one of the missionaries who had come. He found out something that really sparked his interest. The man told him that they need all different types of people on the mission field. My dad told him he was a pilot. The man's face lit up and he said how there was definitely a need for pilots! My dad went away excited and encouraged. Was this God's plan for his life?

That night he talked to my mom. They tossed the idea around in their heads. They thought about the pros and the cons. My dad loved the idea of being a missionary pilot, but the thought of raising support just terrified him. No, he couldn't do that. He was not a public speaker. My mom, on the other hand, tried to encourage him. "It couldn't be that hard," she would say, "you just show your slides and say the same thing over and over again."

Over the next few weeks, my dad wrestled and wrestled with the thought of being a missionary. Was God really calling him to do this? It would mean picking up his family and living a completely different lifestyle. He just didn't know! Meanwhile, my mom didn't think of it much. She really didn't think my dad was that serious. One day, while my dad was out flying, the Lord continued to stir his heart. Knowing he couldn't resist the Holy Spirit any longer, he finally gave in and said, "Yes, Lord." What a peace he had after that! He couldn't wait to get home and tell my mom!

As he burst through the door that evening, he hollered out to my mom, "Praise God, Honey, I'm ready to go!" My mom nearly fell backwards with a stunned look on her face! You mean he was really serious about this whole thing? She had to put a stop to this nonsense real fast!

"What do you mean? We can't just pick up and go! What about the kids? We just bought the house! What about your job at Goodyear? And my piano! I can't leave my piano!" My poor dad! He thought my mom was fine with going and it had been all up to him at this point. His face fell.

After dinner, they decided to do what they should have done all along. With my dad full of discouragement and my mom full of fear, they decided to open up the Bible. But where should they look? They remembered a verse that had to do with sharing the gospel with others, so they decided to go there first. They looked up 2 Timothy 2:2, *"And the things that you have heard from me among many witnesses, commit these to faithful men who will be able to teach others also."* They agreed that as missionaries, they would be doing this very thing. But after reading that verse, my mom's eyes fell on the other page which was the last chapter of 1 Timothy. Starting with verse 6, she read:

*"Now godliness with contentment is great gain. For we brought nothing into this world, and it is certain we can carry nothing out. And having food and clothing, with these we shall be content. But those who desire to be rich fall into temptation and a snare, and into many foolish and harmful lusts which drown men in destruction and perdition. For the love of money is a root of all kinds of evil, for which some have strayed from the faith in their greediness, and pierced themselves through with many sorrows. But you, O man of God, flee these things and pursue righteousness, godliness, faith, love, patience, gentleness. Fight the good fight of faith, lay hold on eternal life, to which you were also **called**..."*

When they reached the word, "called," in the middle of verse 12, they both knew in their hearts that God was calling them to the mission field. Life wasn't about having money or things; it was about doing the will of God. At that point, they both dropped to their knees and surrendered to the calling of their Father God.

My mom and dad sold their home and joined Wycliffe Bible Translators. For the next ten years they served as missionaries, first in Ecuador then in Papua New Guinea. No, my mom couldn't bring her piano, but she made do with a small keyboard. And what about us kids? We feel greatly privileged to have been raised on foreign land!

I Am Calling You

Inspiration received by Holly Placencia

    I am calling you. You're My child and I am calling you. Hear My voice and listen to Me. The road won't be easy, but are you willing to lay down your life? Are you willing to sacrifice the comforts of this life? I am calling you to deny yourself. I am calling you to lose your life for My sake. Lay down your rights so you can serve others. You are a servant; you are My servant.

"Listen to Me, O my people, while I give you stern warnings. O Israel, if you would only listen to Me!"

Psalm 81.8 (NLT)

Watchman on the Wall
by Jill

My sister, Diane, is a 72 year-old retired secretary. We had always been close, and when her marriage of over thirty years had ended, she moved in with me for five years. This was a very special time for both of us. As she healed from her divorce, she decided to join me at my church and eventually accepted the Lord as her personal Savior. During this time, we took Bible classes, attended women's fellowships, and went to prayer meetings together. She shares this story with you, in her own words:

"I was baptized on October 4, 2001, at the age of 55. In January, 2003, a small Bible study group was formed at my church in Southern California. Our pastor led the group. He began and ended each weekly session with prayer, and asked for any praise reports. I didn't usually speak up because of my shyness, but others did. Some people would say they had received a prophecy or words from the Lord. I wished very much to receive that type of spiritual gift. I needed to hear from the Lord directly and prayed that He would use me as His vessel. I wanted to be like Ezekiel, the Watchman on the Wall.

"To my surprise, on the evening of September 4, 2003, the group of about 15 people were asked during the middle of our Bible study to stand up and join hands. Our pastor had been prompted by the Lord to ask someone to speak up with a prophecy. A couple of people had a few words to say, but nothing dramatic. I, indeed, had just received what I believed was a prophecy directly by the Lord, but was too afraid to say it out loud, just in case I was mistaken. After more urging by our pastor and by a lady named Mary Ann (who called me out by name, saying the Lord wanted to use me), I finally agreed to speak out what the Lord was laying on my heart.

"The word was:

'All those in this room will not die before the Rapture!'

"I shrugged my shoulders and stammered around a little trying to explain that it was not me talking but God; I would not have presumed to say such a thing on my own. The people in the room looked shocked. I didn't know what to think. Was it real? Only time will tell, of course."

Diane

My lovely daughter of gentle heart,
A gift to you I now impart.
You think your life is almost through,
But I have come to make you new!

The chaos that is all around
Has brought confusion; kept you bound.
But Truth will always conquer lies,
And I have heard your silent cries.

For your life, I have a plan,
And it will bring great peace, Diane.
Look neither to the left nor right;
Just take My hand and hold on tight.

I'm with you in the morning's dew;
I'm with you in the evening, too.
I never will abandon you;
My love is everlasting, true.

I see you even in the crowd.
I notice you, though you're not loud.
Your quiet manner is your charm.
It's meant to bring you peace, not harm.

You're not invisible to me;
You're a beautiful delicacy.
You're a rare and chosen flower;
And I'm the stem that gives you power.

Take a long and thirsty drink,
And roots will sprout so you won't sink.
Your faith will bud new leaves so green,
If you will choose to, on Me, lean.

Faith comes by hearing with your ears,
And it will chase away all fears.
All doubts and shadows from the past
Will be removed from you, at last!

Happy Birthday, sweet fifty-three.
My gift to you today is *Me!*
May you enjoy forevermore
My love and blessings by the score!

God (Through your loving sister, Jill)

I listen carefully to what
God the Lord is saying,
For He speaks peace to
His faithful people. . .

Psalm 85:8 (NLT)

Neva's Choice...Or God's Purpose?

by Holly

My sister, Neva had been working at the bank for many years. She was tired, she was stressed, and she had some severe health problems. Her rheumatoid arthritis and fibromyalgia made it difficult to get through each day. She wished her hours could be cut back, but a part-time position was not available. Her boss added to the stress by her constant criticisms and insults. She had a lot of pressure to perform at work. On top of all that, she had to commute daily up and down the mountain. She needed more sleep but was never able to get enough. It was becoming more than she could handle. Her new husband of 4 years had compassion on her. One more year, he told her, and she could quit her job. They would be okay financially by then.

It was the beginning of 2017. Christmas and all its craziness was over. The in-laws had come and spent several days up until New Year's Day. Now it was time to go back to work. Was Neva ready for this? Absolutely not! She thought about the year ahead. How would she be able to get through another year? It seemed overwhelming to her.

January 4th she dragged herself to work. She felt terrible--physically, mentally, emotionally. She almost called in sick but decided against it. When she sat down at her desk, ready to start her day at work, she was suddenly jolted by a word she knew was from the Lord! Actually, it was a question. **"What if you were going to die today?"** she heard Him say.

Neva immediately dismissed the thought. "If I die, I die," she said to herself. But as the voice pressed into her thought life, she knew it was the voice of God...and it was a question that demanded an answer. "No," she told the Lord. "I'm not ready to die." She thought of her daughters and granddaughters who still needed her.

Neva managed to get up from her desk, drink a cup of coffee, and eat some fudge. Maybe that would give her some energy. But when she returned to her desk, she fell apart. Her chest started hurting, her arms were heavy, she couldn't focus; she felt flushed. Her mind was in a whirlwind and she had no physical strength left. Something was terribly wrong! A co-worker looked over her way and noticed there was a problem. "Are you okay, Neva?

At that point, she burst into tears! The co-worker rushed Neva out of there and took her to Urgent Care. Soon she found herself in an ambulance, being transported to the hospital. She was suffering from a heart attack!

While in the ambulance, Neva saw a vision. She saw the edge of the world with a beautiful sunrise. The colors seemed to be dancing around; they were vibrant, peaceful, and very very enticing. She knew all her pain and suffering would be gone if she went the way of the light. But once again, she thought of her daughters and granddaughters. She hadn't said goodbye to them; it would be too devastating for them. No, it wasn't her time to die yet. She believed that God was giving her a choice. She purposely turned her head away from the light and decided to stay on this earth a little longer.

Neva stayed in the hospital a few days, then went home to recover. Her loving husband informed her that she would never need to go back to work. They would find a way to make it financially. This was God's way of letting them both know that it was time for Neva to retire and stay at home. She can finally get the rest that her body was crying out for.

A couple months later, the Lord inspired Neva with a poem. She is not a poet by nature; the only way she can write a poem is by the inspiration of the Holy Spirit. Here is her poem:

God's Presence

Busy, busy,
Go, go, go,
What is my purpose?
I do not know.

Kids are grown,
Easy, it should be,
Still wanting to help them,
Because it satisfies me.

From mountain to valley,
Work, work, work.
Juggle other duties,
Living for that perk.

Not listening to my body,
Got to keep up the pace,
Just get stronger meds,
To compete in the race.

Went to work on Jan. 4,
God whispered in my ear,
"Are you ready
For this to be your last day here?"

Barely paying attention,
I nonchalantly replied,
"If I die, I die,
This day will just be brushed aside."

"But wait, are you serious God?
I'm not ready to die!
No, this can't be,
I'm not ready to comply!"

About an hour later,
Strange things began,
Chest pains, heavy arms,
From me my strength ran.

Urgent Care, hospitals,
A fast ambulance ride,
God's comfort and peace,
Never leaving my side.

Heart pains entering,
The 16th hour,
I began to view the world,
In a dark, dismal power.

I saw a beautiful, sunrise vision,
Bright colors dancing in 3D,
It hurt to turn from the sky's wonders,
But I reminded God of my plea.

Compassion overwhelmed me,
My purpose became clear,
As I saw the faces of my girls,
God's grace let me stay here.

By Neva Liudahl 2017

Make Me Lord of Your Life

Inspiration received by Holly Placencia

Seek Me first above all else. Make Me the Lord and center of your life. Trust Me with all of your heart. I will speak to you and show you the way to go. Do not put anyone else first in your life. Keep your thoughts on Me. I will never fail you. Other people will. They will never meet all of your needs. I know what I am doing. I am doing a work in your life. I will fill your mouth with My words. Follow Me with all your heart. Your life may not look like other people's lives. It may not look like the ideal life. But I am in your heart. Make your life entirely about Me. It doesn't have to look like everyone else's life. I have given you life to live and enjoy. Be thankful for what I give you. Be happy with the little things.

"So pay attention to how you hear. To those who listen to my teaching, more understanding will be given. But for those who are not listening, even what they think they understand will be taken away from them."

Luke 8:18 (NLT)

Season's End

by Jill

I was 48. Four years earlier, I had felt called of God to be a foster parent to children who had been abused and/or neglected. Children in this specialized foster program had lived through inexpressible trauma. Foster parents worked very closely with social workers and therapists of these children. The foster parents received special training as a group, and families within the group helped and supported one another, under the direction of the social workers. My job was to love and nurture the children as my own family. And I did!

It was not uncommon for unforeseen situations to come up, or the need for more therapeutic help to arise as the lives of these children unfolded. Also not uncommon was moving these children from one home to another within the group, in an effort to best meet their needs. For instance, I had a little boy for about six months. He joined two other foster children in my home. When it was learned that he wanted, and asked for, a home where he was the only child, it was promptly arranged. That's what he needed to thrive. And I had to love him enough to say goodbye. I had to say goodbye to another a few years later.

Now there was one little one left in my home. I knew she needed "siblings." But circumstances in my own life dictated that it was time to let go of this very special ministry. Through my tears, I let the Lord know that I felt I was not only letting this child down, but I was also letting Him down if I exited this program. How He comforted me immediately by dropping this scripture into my heart from Ecclesiastes 3:1.

"To everything there is a season, a time for every purpose under heaven."

I knew He was telling me everything has a beginning and an end. This season was ending for me, and she would be okay.

And she was! She was placed in another home right away, and her new family ended up adopting her. God sees the beginning from the end. I'm so thankful He is in control!

Earthen Vessels

"I am the Potter - you are the clay."
These words from our Lord still apply today.
His strong, gentle hands still precisely design
Pots of all sizes and shapes He calls, "Mine."

His craftsmanship is the finest that anyone knows,
And the pride He takes in His work really shows.
Each pot is unique in its color and blend,
And the beauty created is awesome, my friend.

But the question remains for me and for you:
"Will we stay on the wheel 'til the potter is through?"
We can leave when we choose even though we're not done,
But we'll look kind of funny, and our color might run.

Now, the thing about pots is, when dropped, they could break;
Or if handled too roughly, a cracked-pot you could make.
Some pots have been out on their own way too long,
And some have been used in a way that is wrong.

When you look at the people of God, won't you see
How fragile and broken some of them might be.
So carefully handle each precious pot,
For God made them Himself, and He loves them a lot!

Jill Kidd

But all who listen to Me will live in peace, untroubled by fear of harm.

Proverbs 1:33 (NLT)

Your Baby Will Be Alright
by Holly

At the beginning of 1988, I was just starting to show my pregnancy. I proudly wore those maternity tops that said "Baby" with an arrow pointing to my stomach! I already had a healthy baby boy and I was looking forward to a second one.

At the time, my husband and I attended a pentecostal church called "Victory Chapel." It wasn't uncommon to have evangelists come in as guest speakers. It also wasn't uncommon for those preachers to spend lots of time praying for the congregation and speaking words of knowledge to individuals in the church. I always looked forward to those special meetings, and I always hoped that maybe I would be one to receive a special word from God.

On this particular Sunday night, the guest preacher was talking about fear. I listened intently. Being only 24 years old and trying to adjust to marriage and family, I had plenty of fears. At the end of the service, the preacher asked everyone to come forward who was struggling with fears of some sort. I went forward along with almost everyone in the entire church! Who doesn't struggle with fear of one thing or another?

As I stood there praying, the preacher came up to me and laid hands on me. I was excited; maybe I would receive a word from the Lord! Then he looked at me and said:

"Your baby is going to be alright."

I went away disappointed that night. I had fears, but none of my fears had anything to do with this baby I was carrying. I had no doubts that this baby would be alright. He probably noticed my baby shirt and realized I was pregnant. He probably assumed that I was fearful about this baby not being born healthy. He probably wasn't really in tune with the Spirit of God. I kind of just blew the whole thing off.

Several months later, we had another evangelist come to our church. By this time, I was really showing my pregnancy. I was due to have the baby soon. At one point, the preacher had the congregation stand up to get ready for prayer. He suddenly pointed directly at me and said:

"Your baby is going to be alright!"

This time I went home scared. Why would two complete strangers say the exact same thing to me? Why do they keep saying my baby will be alright? Will something be wrong with my baby?

August 9th, Benny was born. He had a bowel blockage and had to be operated on the day he was born. We soon found out that he has cystic fibrosis. He has had multiple lung infections and bowel obstructions, many many hospital stays, several surgeries, and a few near-death experiences. Was he really "alright" like those evangelists said he would be?

I choose to say yes he was. I stood on those words many times. They gave me hope through every surgery and through every negative prognosis. I always believed he would be okay, even though outwardly things seemed hopeless. I can relate to the Apostle Paul when he said, *"We are hard pressed on every side, but not crushed; perplexed, but not in despair; persecuted, but not abandoned; struck down, but not destroyed."* 2 Corinthians 4:8,9

Benny became a fighter, and he fought through many difficult times. Today he is 30 years old and yes, he still struggles with his sickness. His body may be weak but his character is strong. He loves the Lord and he shares his testimony with the world. He has truly turned out "alright."

Trust Me

Inspiration received by Holly Placencia

I told you I am watching over you! Don't you realize I know the beginning to the end? That's why I say to trust Me. Your children will learn the same thing. They have to learn to trust Me. They can't depend on you or other people. I see the whole picture! I know what I am doing. You can't waste your time worrying about them. Worry does nothing to help them at all. I hope you realize now that you can trust Me!

"As it is written in the scriptures, '
They will all be taught by God.'
Everyone who listens to the
Father and learns from Him
comes to Me."

John 6:45 (NLT)

Trust and Obey

by Jill

Holly's longtime friend and past mentor agreed to meet with us at 7th Street Park in Yucaipa, California to relate to us her story. I got to the park first and was sitting in my car, waiting for the others to arrive. It wasn't long before Helen pulled in and parked several empty spaces away from me. I had my car window down enjoying the overcast day. Helen didn't hesitate. She quickly approached me and asked if I was Holly's friend. I told her I was. "I knew it!" she exclaimed.

As I got out of my car to greet her, I suggested we walk to a nearby covered picnic table for our interview. She drew me in immediately, and invited me to first come see what she had in her car's trunk- bags full of journals that she had been keeping for many years from her conversations with the Lord! I couldn't help but see the comparison between Helen and Holly. No wonder they hit it off so well! Holly has quite a collection of journals herself!

As we talked and got acquainted, we headed for the picnic table. I couldn't help but to be drawn to Helen. There was something special about her. Holly arrived just as we were sitting down.

Helen began: "This is a divine appointment." As we started chatting, she said it again. The Holy Spirit was so strong in our midst as she began her story, I had trouble keeping my composure! The tears were welling up in my eyes and it was difficult for me to talk, as the presence of the Lord was overwhelming. I noticed both Holly and I were glued to Helen's words, sitting on the edge of our seats as she shared her experiences about hearing from the Lord.

Helen was a nurse. She began her story by telling us about a very special patient she had known for ten years. Miss Walenski lived way out of the way. When Nurse Helen walked up to her place (nothing more than a hut), she was standing out on the porch and, when Helen got out of the car, Miss Walenski said, "I have been waiting for this moment. This is a divine appointment." And she pointed her finger directly at Helen as she spoke to her. She then said, come on in the house, do my eyedrops, and then we'll get down to business. She was single, had never been married, had no kids, no living relatives, and she lived out in the middle of nowhere! Helen began to wonder, "What in the heck have I gotten into!?"

When Helen's patient sat down, she took her Bible and patted it. Using her finger pointed toward Helen again, she said, "Young lady, what you're looking for you'll find all in this book right here. Stop searching and read God's Word." At that time Helen was not yet a Christian. She hadn't been raised in a Christian home and she knew nothing about the Bible. She had never even owned one! In her 30's at this time (she's now 78) Helen went home and bought her first Bible. Now she was committed. She knew she had to read this thing!

Everyday, Miss Walenski gave her assignments. Helen was instructed to call her each day at 1:00 pm and tell her what she read. No excuses! She went to see her once a week because she was her nurse, and she had to do eye drops. When she would go out there, Miss Walenski would tell Helen her whole life's story (Helen's story, that is!). Somehow she knew about her dad and his drinking problem, and she talked about Helen being very sick as a child. Helen had never told her anything about her own life! How did she know all that? Her life wasn't written in this Bible! She repeatedly asked her patient how she knew all about her. Miss Walenski finally told her what she needed to do, "Be quiet! Quit asking questions, sit down, and be still. And God will reveal Himself to you if you really want to know the truth."

So Helen started every day sitting quietly, asking God, if He is real, to show her who He is. A week went by . . . nothing. Miss Walenski just told her, "Be patient. He is patient." It took awhile, but finally she thought she heard Him say:

"Somebody is going to knock at your door. Let them in."

At that time in her life, she never let anyone in her door that she didn't know. But it wasn't long before the doorbell rang. She couldn't believe it! Could this really be happening to her!?

It was the Avon Lady! Well, of course she had to let her in! It turns out that this lady's husband was a Baptist minister. The Avon Lady told Helen that she felt she might be out talking to people who are lost. Helen was utterly astounded! Was this really happening to her? Helen became a customer of the Avon Lady and they became friends.

In the meantime, Helen continued to meet with her patient, Miss Walenski. She was learning to open her eyes and ears to spiritual things. Then she had a dream. Actually, it was a vision of Christ. He simply said:

"Follow Me."

Helen wasn't sure who *He* was, and asked Him, "Who are you?" He replied:

> **"You need to learn who I am. Don't just believe
> what you have heard about Me.
> Some people say bad things about Me that aren't true.
> You need to find out for yourself who I am."**

So that began a search; not only in the Bible, but also in books that have been written on the life and history of Jesus. She consumed herself in finding out who this Jesus was! That's when she truly decided to follow Him. He told her that she needed to meet with Him every single day and listen. That's where she was to get her direction. He told her she needed to **"trust and obey."** When she would get quiet, He would tell her things she needed to do. If she would argue, she told us that He would tell her to:

> **"Stop it; do what you are told."**

She chuckled and explained to Holly and me that she had been quite rebellious back then. She continued her story:

One of the most uncomfortable things she had to do was to go to this particular Calvary Church. After the service the Lord told her:

> **"Trust Me. You must go up to that pastor and pray for him."**

She didn't even know him! She had never been in that church before. She told the Lord, "No." There was this silence, but she was prompted once more:

> **"Trust Me."**

Helen procrastinated, hoping the pastor would leave . . . he didn't! Finally, with much trepidation, she walked up to that pastor, introduced herself, and told him that she felt led of the Lord to pray for him. He was so gracious and said to her, "I can always use prayer." He leaned over towards her, she put her hands on him, and the Holy Spirit prayed for him. Helen, to this day, has no idea what the prayer consisted of. It was a Holy Spirit prayer and it was, evidently, none of her business.

This whole experience was so emotionally draining on Helen that by the time she got out to her car, she told the Lord she couldn't keep doing this. He replied to her:

"You did a good job. You trusted and you obeyed."

"Obedience is what I needed to learn," said Helen, "to trust that He would do it, and that I was to obey even if it didn't make sense to me."

Helen and Miss Walenski by now had formed a true friendship. Miss Walenski continued to mentor Helen for the next ten years. Miss Walenski was 80 when they met. When she had her 90th birthday, she told Helen that she had told the Lord she wanted to live to be 90. She told Helen, don't grieve for me when I'm gone; I've done my job. I'm finished. Now you need to go out and pass on what you've learned. Miss Walenski died the next day.

"She had a direct line," said Helen. "She knew everything! After she died, I have often wondered . . . could she have been an angel?"

Helen has learned well from Miss Walenski. She is, indeed, passing on what she has learned: "Be quiet! Quit asking questions, sit down, and be still. And God will reveal Himself to you if you really want to know the truth."

The Status Quo Has Got To Go!

The stagnant pool of mediocrity is drowning out my soul,
While death, disease, and hopelessness gladly take their toll.
My cries for help are vapor in the still and thickened air;
No one seems to notice or, perhaps, they just don't care.

Life goes on, or else it doesn't, and I vegetate a bit;
I go about the tasks of life; I eat and drink - and sit.
I long for new adventures that would my soul delight,
But the river has no current, and I'd get lost out in the night.

The river *must* be flowing, with a current deep and strong,
If ever it will lift me and carry me along.
Dear God, send rain from up above to freshen and renew,
And cause the river once again to overflow in You.

Wash me once again, Dear Lord, and let the rivers fill;
Let me frolic for awhile as You reveal to me Your Will.
Then let the current sweep me off my feet to unknown places,
As around the bend you take me to meet and greet new faces.

Then as I step upon dry ground, may the waters never end,
But rivers of living water flow from You through me to them.
The status quo has got to go - mediocrity can't win!
God has a river planned for me, and I am jumping in!

Jill Kidd

Let the wise listen
and add to their learning,
and let the discerning get guidance-

Proverbs 1:5 (NIV)

Then God Spoke
by Holly

Yvonne was young when she married Larry. She had just one desire - to stay home and be a wife and mother. Maybe she was being old-fashioned or not keeping up with the times, but she didn't care. Having a career was not for her. She had a husband who could bring in the money while she stayed home to raise their children.

She thought this was a great plan, but it didn't last long. She soon figured out that the instability of her husband's construction jobs required her to get out there and help supplement their income. She loved children, so quite naturally, she decided to teach preschool. This required early childhood development courses that she was able to complete at the community college.

Soon, this became Yvonne's life - teaching preschool, being a wife to Larry, and raising their three boys. Even though their financial situation wasn't the greatest, she was satisfied, her husband was satisfied, and her boys were taken care of.

Then God spoke:

"You need to go back to college."

"What!" Yvonne exclaimed to herself. That's the last thing she wanted to do! But that still, small voice kept speaking to her:

"You need to go back to college."

Over and over again, day after day, night after night, Yvonne kept hearing the same instructions:

"You need to go back to college."

"But I don't want to go to school!" she said aloud one morning.

"Then don't," her husband replied nonchalantly. He couldn't figure out what the big deal was. But Yvonne knew it wasn't her husband prodding her to do this, nor was it her own thoughts. It was the Lord... and she had to make a decision.

Her decision was to obey this prompting from God. At 38, she decided to get a teaching degree. After several years of hard work, she earned teaching credentials in both general education and special education. Eventually, she landed a job as a special education teacher through the local school district.

During this time, though, her husband developed a life-threatening lung disease, COPD. He had to be on continuous oxygen day and night. He wasn't given much time to live. But the health insurance that Yvonne acquired from working as a teacher through the school district made it possible for Larry to receive the care he needed. If she hadn't listened to the prompting of the Holy Spirit to go back to school, he would have never received that health care. As a result, he lived much longer than the doctors had projected-- a full 15 more years! He got to see all his grandchildren born and was able to build a relationship with them - and they adored him.

Yvonne can testify now that God sees the whole picture when we don't. He knew that Larry would become sick and need some good health insurance. He also knew Yvonne would need a good income of her own when He called her husband home. Yvonne just had to step out in faith and be obedient to Him. Her husband is with the Lord now, but at 60 years old, Yvonne still enjoys teaching boys and girls of all ages.

Fix Your Eyes On Me

Inspiration received by Holly Placencia

There are no perfect people around you. People will say and do things you disagree with. Don't let it bother you. It's not your responsibility to change people. Put your eyes on Me. You follow Me. That is your responsibility. Encourage others to follow Me, but don't try to make their decisions for them. They are not in the same place as you. I have put people in your path right now as your mission field. I bring people in your life and I take them away. It isn't something for you to strive about.

When your eyes are fixed on Me, you don't have to be concerned about your future. Spend more time praying and less time trying to figure things out. Spend time with Me. I have all the answers you need. I know your future and I know the plan I have for you. Follow Me and I will unfold that plan. I don't give you the plan and tell you to go make it happen. It happens as you follow Me. People try to take matters into their hands too much. Put matters in My hands and watch what I do. Let Me do the work. All I ask is that you give Me your all.

Surrender to Me completely. Trust Me with all of your heart. Put Me number one in your life. Serve Me and none other. Don't try to please others. You can't. But you can please Me. Be My servant; live to please Me. Surrender all to Me and watch what I do. Don't take matters into your own hands. I will lead as you follow. Soar with the eagles, and don't look down. I will accomplish what I set out to do. Speak My words and go forward. Don't look back and don't look down. Don't look to the right or left. Keep your eyes fixed on Me. I have a plan and a destiny. It will only happen as you seek Me. Make me Lord of your life. Give me 100%!

My child, pay attention to what
I say. Listen carefully to my words.
Don't lose sight of them.
Let them penetrate deep into your heart,
for they bring life to those who find them,
and healing to their whole body.

Proverbs 4:20-22 (NLT)

Their First Date
by Jill

Denise is an up-beat woman who has a radiant smile that invites you to come in to her circle of friends. Her face reflects the hope she has in the Lord today and the assurance that her future is bright because she is in His loving care.

But it wasn't always so. Raised Catholic, she felt trapped in a religion that just did not make sense to her. She often heard the older women talking about how they wished their son or daughter would come back to the Church so they would be assured of an eternity in Heaven. Denise knew the truth about how to get into Heaven. And it wasn't through the "Church." She knew it was only through Jesus, the Son of God. It wasn't Jesus Christ AND the Catholic Church. She knew she wasn't where she needed to be, but leave the Catholic Church!? Unheard of! She had been taught that a Catholic should never attend any other denomination. And she knew it would hurt her parents beyond words if she did. So she just walked away from church altogether.

This is her story about an encounter with God that, unknown to her at the time, was the beginning of a true relationship with her loving Heavenly Father. After hearing her special story, I couldn't stop myself. I told her it sounded to me like "their first date." He was introducing Himself to her. He certainly got her attention. Read on as she continues, in her own words:

"I went into recovery in 1994, so it had to have been in 1995. My daughter was just a toddler, and one night she was just crying and crying and crying, and I just couldn't get her to go to sleep. And one of my friends in recovery was always saying, "Let the God in me greet the God in thee," which is, "His will, not my will." I was so frustrated. I was getting really angry. I was getting really upset. I couldn't do anything to get her to stop crying. I needed to get up early that next morning, and I finally just sat back on my bed and I cried out in sheer desperation, "Let the God in me greet the God in thee!!!

"There was suddenly this humming white light that came down through my head, down through my body. I felt it go all the way down to my toes and back up, and out. I was at peace; my daughter was at peace. She was quiet. She was asleep! I don't know what it meant, but to me it was like God saying:

"I got this!"

"It was a spiritual experience that has left a mark on me. Like, the finger of God came down through my head. It was a humming, white light. My whole body was just: *hummmmmmmmmmm*. Like His power just washed up and out of my whole body. It's amazing. He was just letting me know He's there, saying to me:

"I got this!"

Today, Denise has found her niche at the Assemblies of God Church where she is attending and serving. She sits up front during worship service, unless she's in the balcony, working the slides. She told me that's her favorite spot. When I asked her why, she replied, "because I'm contributing." She's good with computers and is very comfortable working behind the scenes. She comes to the church on Fridays and prepares the slides for Sundays. Her pastor gives her flexibility to be creative. It's something she enjoys and does well. She feels it's the right spot for her. It's a good fit.

Since this "first date" with her Lord, Denise has continued to grow in her relationship with her Savior. She has learned to trust Him and has a new sense of security and a hope for her future that wasn't there before. She shared with me her favorite Bible verse, which says it all:

Surely goodness and mercy
shall follow me all the days of my life;
and I will dwell in the house of the Lord forever.
Psalm 23:6

Be My Valentine

Valentines are lovely, and I send you one today
To let you know I love you more than words could ever say.
Climb upon your Daddy's lap and let Me hold you near.
I'll cradle you within My arms and banish every fear.

No power on Earth can separate or tear you from My arms.
I'm big enough and strong enough to keep you from all harm.
I could just lift and carry you, by force, to sit with Me,
But love by force just isn't love; you wouldn't then be free.

The struggle that is going on within your mind today
Is fought by every woman and man until they find the Way.
No one can escape it; a decision must be made;
I'm handing you the gift of Life - the price already paid!

All you must do is take it and embrace it as your own.
I love you just the way you are, for you're My flesh and bone.
But, never fear, for there is more to tell to you, My love!
I'll mend the brokenhearted and set free My turtle dove!

The chains that bind you tightly will be banished totally
When you decide to take My hand and always follow Me.
You are My heart's desire, and there's one thing I must say:
I long for you, My Valentine. Will you be Mine today?

GOD (Through His servant, Jill Kidd)

The Sovereign Lord has given me
His words of wisdom,
so that I know
how to comfort the weary.
Morning by morning
He wakens me and opens my
understanding to His will.

Isaiah 50:4 (NLT)

God's Presence
by Holly

I was a single mom for many years. I was raising six boys, working full-time, and going to school. My plate was full! But Christmas was coming soon. I was about to have two full weeks off from work and school, and I was looking forward to it! I would finally get the long-awaited and much-needed rest that I so desired. I was also eager to spend some quality time with my kids.

But when Christmas break started, things weren't going as I had planned. The quality time with my kids didn't seem to be happening, my washing machine broke down, and the stress of Christmas was taking its toll on me. Then the final straw happened just a couple days before Christmas.

My teenage son, Benny, asked if he and his friend, Jose, could use the van to go to Del Taco. Benny only had a driver's permit at that time, but Jose had a driver's license and he would be the one driving the van. I couldn't see any harm in them taking the van since Del Taco was no more than a mile away from my house. So I gave them my permission.

Well, that was a mistake! Not long after they left, I received a phone call from Benny. "Mom, Jose flipped the van!" What?! How in the world did that happen? He started explaining where they were at and I realized they were nowhere near Del Taco! They had decided to take a little detour up the mountain road to see where it went. (I have no doubt this was my son's idea and his friend went along with it.) Evidently, they were driving a little too fast coming down the mountain road and lost control on some loose gravel. When I arrived, I found my van upside down and completely ruined! Some cops were writing a report while the two boys stood there completely unharmed, one chatting away about what happened (my son), and the other one so ashamed he couldn't even lift his head.

My head was in a whirlwind! This was the last thing I needed now! That night I went to my room and sat quietly before God with my Bible on my lap. I was tired, stressed out, and overwhelmed with everything. I finally blurted out, "Lord, when can I ever get some rest?!" Not knowing where to look, I just opened my Bible randomly to Exodus, Chapter 33. My eyes fell immediately to verse 14, which said,

"The Lord replied,
'My Presence will go with you, and I will give you rest.'"

Wow! God heard my prayer and answered me directly! His answer was specific and exactly what I needed to hear. I realized at that time that rest doesn't come through having perfect circumstances; it comes by spending time in His presence. That night I had the presence of the Lord and He gave me peace and rest. My circumstances were crazy; my life was not at all running smoothly. But I could enjoy Christmas and have peace of mind because God's presence was with me. And He gave me the rest I so needed and desired!

Give Up Your Rights

Inspiration received by Holly Placencia

My child, I know you love Me and want to please Me. Come to Me and I will give you rest. I will give you peace and joy. Joy does not come from the world. It does not come from worldly wisdom. Do you want to live a mediocre life? Then listen to the wisdom of this world. It's not all bad. It may give you a boost or a decent life. Or do you want to really live life? A life full of joy and excitement? Then deny yourself, take up your cross and follow Me.

You have rights. You can demand your rights if you want. It may empower you a little bit. You may feel good about yourself for a time. But it will also bring inner turmoil. You have a right to be angry and bitter. You can hang on to that right if you want to. Or you can give it up. Can you change what other people do and what they think? You can speak the truth but you cannot change them. Can you change the past? Lay down your rights, lay down your expectations, lay down your fears. Do you really want My way? It's different from the world.

My way is complete surrender. My way is forgiveness and giving up your rights. My way is loving others in spite of what they do. My way is seeing past the wrong and evil and looking for the good. I am very patient and kind with people. I forgive offenses. I believe in people and I encourage the good. I overlook many faults and I speak words of life and truth. The truth convicts people. My kindness leads to repentance. I don't speak to the outward appearance. I speak to the heart. I understand people and their hurts. I am longsuffering. I don't give up on people. I speak to the heart.

Stop looking to the outward appearance. Don't give up on people. Love them like I do. I will fill you with My love so you can love them. It's not impossible to have joy. It all comes together. When you are filled with the Spirit of God, it all produces love, joy, peace, patience, goodness, faithfulness, kindness, gentleness, and self-control. Watch what happens when you lay down your burdens. Carry nothing! Lay it all down. People can't solve your problems! Empty yourself so I can fill you.

"And so, my children, listen to
Me, for all who follow
My ways are joyful.
Listen to My instruction
and be wise. Don't ignore it.
Joyful are those who
listen to Me. . ."

Proverbs 8:32-34 (NLT)

A Servant of the Most High God!

by Jill

I had worked as a secretary all my adult life. However, ever since I was born again at the age of 33, I had a desire to work in the ministry full time. At one point, I was offered a job as a secretary at the church where I was saved. I would have loved to take them up on the offer, but the position didn't pay very well. My children were still school age and the timing wasn't right. So I kept my job as a legal secretary, but at the same time I involved myself in ministry in other ways, continually growing in the Lord. It wasn't long before I was teaching a Sunday school class and attending classes in evangelism and anything else the church offered.

When I was in my late 40's, a dozen or so of my friends and I had the opportunity to start a new fellowship in a very oppressed part of a neighboring community. The pastor was our only paid staff. What a joy to experience all God was doing among us there! How I wanted to quit my job and plunge in head first! Of course I still had to support myself, so I kept working my job and served on a volunteer basis at the church as much as I could. But God knew my heart. After all, He should! He has promised to give us the desires of our hearts. The best news is that He makes us new creations, and actually puts new desires into our hearts! *His* desires!

Then I turned 50. (Where does the time go!?) The desire to go full time into ministry was still there. I heard the Lord tell me:

"Get out of debt in five years."

I said, "OK!" I had a few credit cards and leased a nice car, but I was not over my head; it was all manageable. I was making good money and could pay my bills. But I knew I had heard from the Lord on this, so ... I got out of debt in five years!

At age 55, the Lord spoke to me about all this again. He said:

"It's time to get down there and help that man."

My pastor was still taking care of everything by himself. His wife was the children's pastor, and they needed help in the office. That, I knew how to do! I was ready and was very excited, but needed some questions answered. At the time, I was the treasurer of our church, and I knew we could not afford me. So I asked of the Lord how I was supposed to support myself under these conditions. He dropped this idea on me:

"Take out your retirement fund and use it to support yourself for now."

I had been working for the school district nine years, so my retirement fund was available to me. I went to my pastor and his wife to discuss all this. They agreed that I had heard from the Lord, and welcomed me aboard. The pastor felt that by the time my retirement fund ran out, the church would have grown enough to support me as well as them. Against advice from most everyone, I arranged to retire and take my retirement money with me.

I remember the day I went into the school where I worked to announce my decision to retire to my supervisor. I was a little nervous and knew everyone would be asking me exactly what I would be doing. I wanted to be ready with an answer. I knew I would be taking care of the church office needs, but I also knew it would be much more. It would be true ministry! If only I could have a title of sorts to explain it to my co-workers at the school. My pride got in the way a little, I suppose, but I just didn't want them to think I was going to merely be the church secretary. So, as I was walking into the building, mustering up my courage to announce my retirement, I asked the Lord what my title was... so I could explain it all better.

Oh my goodness - let me tell you what happened! He spoke to me in the deepest part of my being with a deep, resounding voice that filled my entire body. I did not hear it with my ears, but I heard it with my whole being!

"YOU'RE A SERVANT OF THE MOST HIGH GOD!"

Okay! That was all I needed! He had spoken to me, loudly and clearly, and all my fears and doubts about doing this instantly vanished! I knew in my heart that was the best title I could ever have. But I didn't tell them. It was no longer necessary, nor would they understand.

As it turned out, that retirement money lasted almost a year. The church could only afford to pay me a small amount by that time. But more money came my way that was totally unexpected. It came from many different directions, and the timing was perfect. By the time all that ran out, the church was able to pay me a small, but adequate, salary. I didn't need much. Remember, the Lord had instructed me to get out of debt. If I had not, I wouldn't have been able to survive financially. I also would have missed out on the most exciting adventure of my life... so far!

Send Me!

There are so many who are hurting
Who haven't found the Way.
In their blindness, they are stumbling -
Bruised and battered - day by day.

Are they on the path *You've* carved for them?
Is this their journey's end?
By the Grace of God, I know it's not!
You've made *me* to be their friend.

For I've been there; I know the path.
It's full of ruts and holes.
Danger lurks 'round every bend
And weakens hearts and souls.

Oh, use me, Lord, to point the lost
Toward Safety, Peace, and Joy.
Let them see in me the Love of God;
This servant, Lord, deploy.

Here am I, Lord, send me!
Send me!

Jill Kidd

"My sheep
listen to My voice;
I know them,
and they follow Me."

John 10:27 (NLT)

The Best "Yes"
by Jill

Brenda has heard God speak to her many times, but there is one time she clearly remembered Him giving her some very specific instructions about what He wanted her to do.

There was a worship pastor position opening at her church. This was something she wanted. She believed she had been waiting her entire life for a position like this and, certainly, this was why they had been led to this church. This had to be it!

God simply spoke to her and said:

"I'm not going to give the worship pastor position to you.
I have something else I want you to do."

He said:

"I want you to help the person I am sending.
Be there for him and assist him.
Help him transition into the position."

She was obedient and, even though she really wanted that position, she obeyed the voice of the Lord.

Sometime later, the Lord spoke to her again. He wanted her to take the children's church position at the church. Her heart was pricked by the Holy Spirit. She knew this was God calling her back and stirring an old ministry up where she used to serve. By this time, she was established on the worship team, and loved what she was doing. They had a choir. They were preparing to do a recording soon. She was happy singing on the worship team. But God had other plans. The children's church leader had recently resigned and she had experience in this area, but had not told anyone. She began discussing this with the Lord because, well, she wasn't really thrilled about this idea. She knew, however, that it never does any good to argue with God about something He wants you to do. He always wins. Then He said something that really got her.

He said:

"I want you to teach my smallest of sheep."

How could she say no? So she asked God for help. She asked for a team of people. She was specific. She asked Him to put men on her team who would help her. She asked for Spirit-filled people who would lead with her.

Then she had to meet with her pastor. She prepared her program to present to him. When she laid out her one-year program in front of him he said, "This is it!" They put a call out for volunteers and they came quickly. Men and women joined the team. God sent her Spirit-filled leaders. For the next couple of years, she lead the ministry with these people by her side. They saw children's lives changed. They saw kids receive Christ for the very first time. They watched them raise their hands and praise God together. Many of them have continued to serve God even today. Some have become worship leaders; some have gone on missions trips to foreign lands; several are serving in various other church ministries. The legacy lives on because she chose to obey the voice of the Lord.

She could have said no. She could have ignored it. She chose to say yes. When we accept the calling He has for us and walk in His will, incredible things happen. She's no longer called to operate in this capacity. She believes that season of her life has passed. She sees now that God had called her to work in the children's ministry so He could prepare her to be a worship pastor in Santa Paula a few years later. She was eventually to do what she believed and knew in her heart she had been training to do all her life. Her training just wasn't complete. She wasn't ready. If she had not taken on that children's ministry, she feels she would not have developed the skills she needed to become a worship pastor. She would have missed the joy of watching the smallest of God's sheep come to Christ and develop into the beautiful people He desired them to be.

Brenda knows now from personal experience, the best "yes" you will ever say is **YES** to Jesus!

Do It My Way

Inspiration received by Holly Placencia

Continue to seek Me. I will lead you. Pray and seek My face and you won't be steered in the wrong direction. My ways are higher than your ways. Most people don't know My ways. Most people don't seek Me. Don't rely on people to show you the way. They really don't know. They can only guess or go by their own experiences. I do know the way and I know what's right. Doing what's right is not easy. It's going against the grain of what your human nature dictates. I have a plan for you and I won't steer you wrong. But do things My way and don't be in a hurry. Don't try to figure it all out and make your own plans. Be patient and loving and kind. Be forgiving. This is My way.

"But blessed are your eyes,
because they see;
and your ears,
because they hear."

Matthew 13:16 (NLT)

Sherry's Dream
by Jill

Sherry was a California girl, born and raised - until she had that very unusual dream . . . the dream that would change her life forever!

She told me that she considered herself to be an atheist during this season of her life. She believed Jesus was a man that lived a long time ago in history, but to believe He was the Son of God just seemed too made up; too far-fetched . . . until that night Jesus came to her in a dream and told her:

"Sell what you own and move East."

It was such a powerful dream, that she knew she had truly heard from God Himself. He was real, and she was determined to obey. She understood it would mean leaving her mom and dad and all the family - leaving all she knew! But she didn't care. She was convinced she had heard from God. He hadn't told her where to go exactly; just to head East.

She woke her husband to tell him about it. He thought about it for a minute, and then said, "Okay!"

They put their home on the market the next day and it sold within two weeks! And, it sold for $130,000 *more* than they were asking!! The buyer wanted it really bad, and asked them if they could be out in two weeks. They said they could. They saw all this as a sign to them that God was, indeed, sending them East.

They traded in both their vehicles and bought a truck with a camper shell. They put a mattress in the bed of the truck - and headed East. The next two months were quite an adventure. They didn't know where they were going, but it was exciting! Really fun! Of course, their 10-year-old son enjoyed it tremendously. They saw the Grand Canyon and the sand dunes, and went through Vegas. He thought that was cool. It was a vacation of a lifetime!

They went to 32 states, but they never found what they would be calling "home" until they went up the East Coast from Florida and ended up in Vermont. Sherry's husband, Jon, had a sister and a brother living in that area. The brother had always been a delinquent growing up - was into drugs and other bad things. Now, however, he was really different! He told them he was attending church and invited them to come. Coming from him, they said, "Absolutely! We will go with you and support you at your church." They weren't thinking, "This might be our church."

So they went, and fell in love with the people there. Sherry told me that the pastor talked with her for two solid hours. It was just amazing, as he was just like any other guy. Everyone was so friendly, they agreed to attend there for the three weeks they were planning on staying with Jon's sister. It wasn't long, however, before they decided, this is it! This is where they were supposed to be! So they looked for a house in the area. They found one in New Hampshire, just 30 minutes from the church.

Within two months, Sherry, her husband, Jon, and their son, Ian, all became born-again believers in Jesus!

In Sherry's words, "All these little signs just opened up to us, right before us. Everything was a sign to us. All because I heard from God in a dream. He caused everything to open up for us. He gave us the money to do this, to have that once-in-a-lifetime trip with our son. And we all got saved!"

Childhood

I remember the games from my childhood;
Like "kick-the-can," "7-Up," "tag,"
Or racing for kingdoms on hilltops,
Where the winner would raise up their flag.

"Red Rover, Red Rover," we all yelled,
"Send Susie or Tommy right over!"
Charging as fast as they could they would run
Through the grassy field, covered in clover.

All the hands clasped to prevent them
From breaking through chains made of fingers;
The laughter, the thrill of the moment,
Now, as a memory, lingers.

The feel of the wind while running,
The smell of the freshly cut grass;
Daydreams and hopes for the future,
No doubt, would *all* come to pass.

But childhood somehow escaped me,
As fear and mistrust replaced games.
Days run into days with no meaning,
And numbers now replace names.

"Become once again like a child,"
My Father above does beseech,
For in faith, there is freedom from worry,
And in trust, new heights I can reach!

Fresh joy and adventure He gives me,
As I learn to obey His Will;
Now gladly I will proclaim Him,
For *my* Daddy is *"King of the Hill!"*

Jill Kidd

"And the seeds that fell on the good soil represent honest, good-hearted people who hear God's Word, cling to it, and patiently produce a huge harvest."

Luke 8:15 (NLT)

The Peace of God
by Holly

"Which story do you want me to tell?" Margie asked us as we sat down to interview. "I have so many of them."

"Tell me one where you really feel like God spoke to your heart," I answered.

"That would have to be the one about my daughter," Margie replied. She closed her eyes as she began to relive the experience she had with her daughter many years ago.

Jessica was an energetic, enthusiastic, 13-year-old soccer player. She was a go-getter, and rarely stopped to rest. That's why Margie thought it was odd to come home from work one day and see Jessica lying in front of the TV. She said her side hurt. Her dad had taken her to the doctor earlier that day, but the doctor said there was nothing wrong, that she was fine. But as the evening came, Jessica's pain intensified. Margie decided to take her to urgent care; there was something definitely wrong!

The doctor at urgent care looked at her and said she might have mono. Or it could be leukemia. Of course that was the last thing on Margie's mind! This had to be something minor that she would get over soon. But after the blood test was taken, it was confirmed that, yes, this was leukemia.

Jessica's first question was, "Am I going to die?" Of course, Margie didn't know how to answer that one. We're all going to die someday; it just depends on the time frame. Jessica's dad did some research on leukemia and found out that it is treatable and it's not necessarily a death sentence. This gave some comfort to the whole family.

So they took her to the hospital where she had to stay for 3 to 4 weeks. They put in a central line and treated her with IV drugs and chemotherapy. They also had to give her radiation treatments to her head because of the chance of the cancer spreading to the brain.

All of this put Margie in a whirlwind. She didn't know what was going to happen to her daughter. But the worst was yet to come. During all this treatment, Jessica's bowel burst open! Poison was spreading throughout her body. The doctors had to do emergency surgery. No one knew if she would make it.

This is when Margie started praying really hard. "Please, Lord, let her live! Or... take me instead!" she pleaded with God. And God answered her prayer. It wasn't an audible voice that she heard and it wasn't even with specific words spoken to her heart; it was just the peace of God. God's peace came over Margie and she knew that everything was going to be okay. She knew that her daughter was going to live!

Meanwhile, Jessica had to wear two ostomy bags, one for the large intestines and one for the small intestines, in order to drain out the poisons in her system. Then a bacteria developed! Pseudomonas is a very aggressive bacteria that's extremely hard to fight against. Now the odds were definitely against her! At that point, though, her body did an amazing thing. It formed a "fistula," which is an abnormal passage between two organs. The poisons from her bowel entered this passage and flowed to the bacteria and killed it! What modern medicine was not able to do, the body did on its own!

Jessica spent two and a half years in and out of the hospital. But she eventually recovered and her leukemia has been in remission for many years now. Today she's a vibrant, active, and caring young woman in her 30's.

Margie knew her daughter would live. God spoke to her heart in a way she couldn't explain . . . and she just knew it!

Pray With People
Inspiration received by Holly Placencia

Everyone around you needs Me. People with un-Christian attitudes need to turn to Me. You are to shine your light wherever you go. Pray with people. You want prayer partners? You will have them when you pray with people. Pray with the weak Christians and pray with the strong. Pray with the unbelievers. Pray with people every day. Become a prayer warrior. Don't look around at what others are doing or not doing.

I have placed you on a mission field. Ask people what they need prayer for and they will tell you. Pray for them. I am the one who answers prayer. I hear the prayers of My people. I am not deaf and I don't ignore people. I will give you prayer partners. Some will be weak in the faith and some will be strong. The more you pray, the more your faith will grow strong. I am not blind to your needs. I know everything that you do. I see where you go. I know your life. I am in control. Let Me be more in control. Let Me lead you. Pray without ceasing. Don't let anyone else control your thoughts and your affections. Let Me fill your mind completely. Seek Me with all your heart. Pour out your heart to Me and I will answer you.

. . . You must all be quick to listen, slow to speak, and slow to get angry.

James 1:19 (NLT)

He Knows My Name!
by Jill

What a year! Could it get any worse!? It seemed one thing after another hit - all a "10" on the Richter Scale! Some things were so difficult, I even questioned God and His love. I found myself wondering if I really wanted to go on with the Lord. Maybe I should just walk away! I tell you the truth, when I actually considered that alternative, I remember thinking, "But where will I go? Who else can I trust with my life?" That was when I made the decision to praise Him anyway and go on trusting Him.

It was in the autumn of that year, 1996, that I went to an evening service at a church I was attending at the time. We had a guest speaker who moved in the gift of prophecy among other gifts. The service was awesome and when the time had come, he dismissed us. As everyone was standing up to leave, he suddenly stopped us, saying, "Wait a minute! Everyone please take your seats again. The Lord just reminded me of something I forgot about."

Then he went on to explain that on his flight here, the Lord told him there would be a woman in the congregation by the name of "JILL," and he had a message for her.

I was flabbergasted! He asked if there was, indeed, someone by that name here. As soon as I recovered from my shock, I went forward to meet him at the altar. First, he confirmed that my name was Jill. Then he told me, "You have had a very rough year this year, haven't you?" I nodded.

Then I answered decisively, "Yes, I have!"

He said, "But you decided to praise the Lord anyway, didn't you!?" Again, I nodded, taken slightly aback that he used those exact words.

He continued, "The Lord wants me to tell you that it was a test. And you passed. And the Lord is going to reward you. It will be a financial reward. Not a small amount. If someone gives you $100, that's not the reward. It is much bigger than that. And it will come before Christmas." I stood there, stunned, as we were dismissed.

Mom went on to be with the Lord December 19, 1996. Her funeral was the day before Christmas. I ended up inheriting my parents' home. It was paid for. All I had to pay was space rent at the wonderful mobile home park where they had lived for many years. Even that was low because I was grandfathered in at the rate they had been paying.

The Lord had begun way back then to make it financially possible for me to eventually quit my job as a school secretary when I turned 55, and become "a servant of the Most High God" on a full-time basis!

Walking in His Light

When depression overcomes me and my heart no longer sings,
That's the time to turn to Jesus and ask why.
For the Lord, in His great wisdom, wants to purify my mind,
And there's something in my life which I deny.

So He puts me through the fire; it's okay - I understand -
It's the dross in me He wants to burn away.
The imperfection's rising to the top so I can see it
And surrender it to Jesus day by day.

Oh, Glory, Hallelujah; For He burns away the dross
And, even though the fire gets quite hot,
The flames will never touch me, for it only serves to cleanse,
And I come out the purer - without spot.

He restores to me by birthright; my dignity; my worth; my life!
He wraps me in a fresh, clean robe of white.
There's nothing more to be ashamed of - I no longer need to hide -
For I'm walking in the sunshine of His light!

Praise the Lord, for I am walking in His light!

Jill Kidd

"Listen as Wisdom calls out! Hear as understanding raises her voice! . . . Listen to Me! For I have important things to tell you. Everything I say is right, for I speak the truth and detest every kind of deception."

Proverbs 8:1, 6, 7 (NLT)

God Had a Plan
by Holly

It was December 2003, the year I celebrated my 40th birthday. It was also when I earned my bachelor's degree in liberal studies. How did I do that while raising six boys by myself and working full time? I give all the credit to God! He helped me every step of the way and gave me the strength I needed.

I had worked hard, and I was ready to take a little break from school for a few months. The credential program would be the next step, but I decided to put that off for the time being. Besides, it just didn't feel right to go into the credential program. I didn't have a peace about that. I couldn't understand why not, though. I knew from the beginning I wanted to be a teacher. I considered going for middle school math or English, but eventually I settled on teaching elementary school. So why didn't I have a peace about going through the credential program? That's an absolute necessity in order to be a teacher!

I coasted through the next few months, enjoying my time off. That spring, I proudly graduated with my college class. At the same time, we celebrated the high school graduation of my oldest son, Joseph. One down, five more to go!

But what was I supposed to do next? I just didn't know! That summer, I was at church talking with a person I was just slightly acquainted with. She was a public school teacher, and she told me how much money she was making. Wow, I remember thinking how it was so much more than what I was making as a preschool teacher!

"That's it," I told myself, "I'm going to get my credential!" Classes started in two weeks and I had a lot to do to prepare for it. I had to get recommendations, transcripts, fill out the application, sign up for classes, buy the books, and who knows what else. Whew! Those two weeks flew by like a whirlwind!

But there was one big problem. God was not in this at all. He had not given me peace about it, but I went ahead and did it on my own anyway. In my mind, it just seemed like the next logical step I needed to take to becoming a teacher. But those two weeks of preparation were extremely stressful for me. From day one, my insides were turning and I felt sick to my stomach.

When classes started, things got even worse. I was totally overwhelmed by the work I was required to do and couldn't see any possible way I could ever get it done. My mind was in a fog, and I continued to feel sick to my stomach. Completing this program seemed like an impossible task to me! I wondered how I was able to do all the work I had done to earn my degree, yet I wasn't able to do this.

After two weeks, I couldn't take it anymore, and I decided to drop out. I felt like a huge weight was lifted off my shoulders! My stomach ache was gone! Yes, I had wasted a bunch of time and money trying to do things my way, but how thankful I was to be back in the will of God! This was a time when God used his peace (or lack of it) to speak to me. But the story is not over yet.

I still didn't know what I was supposed to do next. I just knew what I wasn't supposed to do! So I called the school and set up an appointment with the counselor. It was another two months before I could see this lady. Finally the day came for my appointment. I asked her, "What else can I do with my bachelor's degree besides be a teacher?" (I thought teaching was out of the question by then).

She proceeded to tell me several ideas of how I could use my degree, all of which I don't remember now. Then she said something that I had never thought of, but that spoke directly to my heart. This woman was not even a Christian, but God used her to speak to me.

"You could teach special ed.," she said nonchalantly.

"That's it!" I said excitedly. I knew at that moment, that God was calling me to special education. There was no special education program at that college; that's why it was never mentioned or considered as an option. The counsellor scribbled a few numbers down on a piece of paper and sent me on my happy way. She was happy because I was happy, but she had no idea that God had just used her to speak to me. Can God sometimes speak to you through an unbeliever? You bet He can!

It wasn't until February of the next year that I started the special education program at a completely different college. I ended up getting two credentials in special education and a master's degree. Today I teach severely disabled children and I love it. When God makes the plan, He makes all things possible!

Be Who You Are Called To Be

Inspiration received by Holly Placencia

Let your life be an open book. Do not be afraid. Speak the truth. Go out in boldness. Say the things I tell you to say. Be the person I created you to be. Be the one I have called you to be. Do what I have called you to do. Don't be intimidated or afraid of anything. Now is the time to act. Today is the day of salvation. Don't wait until tomorrow or one day in the future. I have called you, and I need you to take action. Stop cowering in fear. Step out and be obedient. There's not much time left and I want to use you for my kingdom.

"My child,
listen and be wise:
Keep your heart
on the right course."

Proverbs 23:19 (NLT)

Gentle Chastisement From a Loving Father
by Holly

Sandra and I have been friends for nearly 40 years. I was 16 and she was 19 when we first met. She was always just one step ahead of me in everything. The first thing she taught me was how to ride a horse! I never became very good at that. Next, she taught me how to drive. I remember clutching the wheel in terror as she calmly guided me down the road the very first time I sat in the driver's seat. She was married before me, and she told me all about married life. She started having kids before me, and she taught me everything she knew about babies and children. She became a professional roller skater, and she taught me how to roller skate. She hit menopause before I did and, yes, she taught me everything I need to know about menopause!

Sandra has faced several trials and heartaches in her life, but her Christian faith has always been strong. She has never wavered in her beliefs. Not only did she teach me the facts of life, she was also the one who invited me to a Bible study that had a tremendous impact on my life. As a teenager, I soaked in every word at this Bible study, and I grew spiritually by leaps and bounds. Sandra has definitely been a positive influence on my life!

A few days ago, Sandra and I had lunch together. I asked her the question I've been asking a lot of people lately, "Have you ever felt God speak to you directly?"

"Yes, several times," she answered.

"Tell me about one of them," I prodded.

Then she told me a story of when she was just 15 years old. She was at that very vulnerable age when girls are discovering who they are, and are desperately trying to fit in. Sandra was no different. She was never in the "popular" group. She was more like in the "invisible" group. She just blended in with the crowd and was one of the unknowns. At times, though, she would be picked on by the other girls. She doesn't really know why.

One day, a friend invited her to a party. There would be drinking and craziness that Sandra was not accustomed to, but... the popular kids would be there and, wow, she was actually invited! Maybe this would be her chance to fit in with the other kids. Being raised in a Christian home, she was hesitant at first, but went ahead and agreed to go.

At the party, she was surrounded by noise, laughter, and drunkenness. Somebody handed her a can of beer, which she took but didn't drink at all. She was beginning to feel very out of place. Next thing she knew, someone bumped into her and beer spilled all over her clothes. And this was supposed to be fun?

She had to find a bathroom. The party was being held outside, so she had to go inside the dark, empty house. All alone in that quiet house, she suddenly heard a voice that permeated throughout her entire being:

"WHAT ARE YOU DOING HERE?"

The voice was stern, yet there was no anger or condemnation in the voice at all. In fact, the words were said out of pure love and compassion. She knew it was her Father God speaking to her, and she knew she had to get out of there!

Sandra ran outside to find her friend. "I have to leave!" she said in a very urgent tone. Her friend couldn't understand what the big deal was, but since Sandra was so insistent, she arranged to have someone take her home.

What relief she felt when she finally arrived home. She knew this was not the lifestyle she was meant to have. She made a decision that day to always follow the Lord and not follow the crowd.

I'm glad she made that decision. My life would have been different without Sandra's positive influence on me!

Bait

Glitter and glitz,
All shiny and bright,
Blind us from truths
Of what's wrong and what's right.

Temptation is pretty
And catches the eye.
It draws us in quickly,
Then leaves us to die.

Gain wisdom and knowledge
Before it's too late.
Heaven is waiting,
So, don't take the bait!

Jill Kidd

*Come and listen to my counsel.
I'll share My heart with you
and make you wise.*

Proverbs 1:23 (NLT)

God's Love
by Holly

Stephanie grew up in church. She was in church every Sunday that she can remember, not to mention midweek services and prayer nights. And don't forget those revival weeks... she would be in church every night until late! From a very young age, she knew God was real; she saw the evidence with her very own eyes! She saw people being healed of their ailments and addictions, she witnessed demons being cast out of people who were oppressed, and she saw many people come to the Lord with their lives being changed. Oh yes, Stephanie certainly believed in God!

But although she saw God as her creator, she questioned how loving and caring He was. Who was this God of love that the pastor so often preached about from the pulpit? Why did so many people praise Him in countless testimonies that she had heard? Why wasn't He a God that cared about her? Why did He turn His back on her? Stephanie's experience did not lead her to believe in a God of love at all. For, although she was being raised in church, she was also being sexually abused.

From the age of seven until eleven, Stephanie was molested by a person whom she was really close to. This happened on a weekly basis, oftentimes more. Many mundane situations became moments that terrified her. She felt dirty and worthless and too ashamed to tell anyone. In fact, as a child, the shame it created was sometimes harder to handle than the act itself! She considered telling someone, but she thought of all the devastation it would cause everyone around her. So she told no one. Five years she suffered in silence, becoming more and more withdrawn. She didn't talk, she didn't smile, she just existed.

As the years went by, Stephanie felt more and more invisible to those around her. As far as she was concerned, God had turned His back on her. He didn't care about this little girl who was hurting so badly. He wasn't the loving, caring Father she had heard countless stories about. It felt like He was cold and callous, creating beauty only for it to be destroyed.

Thankfully, one day when Stephanie was eleven years old, the sexual abuse came to an end. Stephanie's mom confronted her about something that she sensed, and Stephanie confirmed that she had been a victim of molestation.

Immediately the molester was confronted and from that time on, never touched her again. Eventually, the molester repented and got his heart right with God. To this day, it remains a secret between Stephanie, her parents, and the molester.

In all of this, much forgiveness had to take place, and did take place. But sadly, the damage had already been done. The hole that was created from being molested was so vast that it felt like nothing could repair it. Stephanie became more and more introverted, constantly fighting feelings of despair. Her resentment towards God increased. How could He claim to love her so much yet allow her to endure so much heartache?

All these emotions came crashing down on her one dark day at 18 years old. Stephanie was home alone on a Saturday afternoon while the rest of her family was at a barbeque. She didn't particularly like being around people, so she chose to stay home and get the laundry done. Her mind raced with one despairing thought after another as she washed her clothes in the garage. Then it happened-- the thought entered her mind to kill herself! She looked up and saw an extension cord hanging from the beams in the garage. All she needed was something to stand on; she could hang herself and end her life! She knew suicide was wrong, but she just couldn't go on anymore.

But God saw Stephanie and intervened in her life at that very moment. Just as she went inside to find a chair, her mom walked into the house. She came home unexpectedly because she forgot something. When Stephanie saw her mom, she broke down and spilled her guts. She told her everything she had planned to do. Her mom prayed for her and they cried together. Her mom would not let her out of her sight the rest of the evening. Seeing her mom was exactly what she needed at the time to forever shake those thoughts of suicide.

The next day, Stephanie went to church, determined to find some answers. She stood up during praise and worship, closed her eyes and lifted her hands up to God. She pleaded with God to show her His love. At that moment, she didn't care if anyone else ever loved her; she just needed to know that God did. Suddenly, she felt arms wrap around her and hug her so tightly. She was shocked, and immediately opened her eyes so she could push away whoever was touching her. But there was no one there! She continued to feel the arms around her, and a warmth came over her from the top of her head to the tip of her toes!

She closed her eyes again to soak up the feeling. Then she heard a whisper:

*"I love you so much. You are more
precious to me than you will ever know!"*

God gave Stephanie exactly what she needed. From that point on, she would never again live her life in despair. It hasn't always been easy; there have been many ups and downs. But whenever those feelings of shame and worthlessness come over her, she calls out to her heavenly Father who answers her immediately. He wraps His arms around her and whispers:

"Be still.

You are safe.

I love you so much.

You are more precious to Me than you will ever know!"

Fight With the Sword of the Spirit

Inspiration received by Holly Placencia

There's a battle for your soul. Don't give in. Fight for what's right. Put on the full armor of God. Use the sword of the Spirit to fight back. Use the Word of God. It's a battle but you can come out victorious. The enemy wants to tear you down. But I have plans for you. I have plans you don't even know about yet. Don't give in to the enemy. Be strong. Fight against the attacks. I have given you My Spirit. He lives in you. He is your helper.

Allow My Spirit to fight your battles. Don't spend your time on things that tear you down. I have a job for you. Put on your battle clothes and go to war! You can't sit around and look back. There's too much at stake. There are things I need you to do. Go forward and march. Take charge of your life and go forward. There's no more time to waste. I have plans. Don't fall for the schemes of the evil one. He wants to hold you back. But there is work to be done. Go forward, and don't turn back. Don't look back, or you will be immobilized.

*"Come here and listen,
O nations of the earth.
Let the world and everything
in it hear My words."*

Isaiah 34:1 (NLT)

The Phone Rang
by Holly

Pastors Greg and Gail are the pastors at Church on the Hill in Redlands, California, where Jill and I attend church. We sat with Pastor Gail one day and heard her stories. We listened as she told us about her dating relationship with Pastor Greg . . . way back when. She told us that she had felt God speak to her several times about him, confirming that he was God's will for her.

Christmas Eve during this dating season was so special for Gail. She had just spent a wonderful evening with Greg. They had been friends for a while and were now in the beginning stages of a deeper relationship. This night was extra special because . . . this was the night Gail received her first kiss from Greg! That kiss meant the world to Gail! She took that kiss seriously. With all the feelings she had for Greg, and all the prayers she had prayed to God, she really believed that now there was a future in store for her and Greg.

But the odd thing was, Greg didn't call her after that. Not at all that week, or the next, or the next. Three weeks had gone by and no call from Greg! Gail was confused. Why wasn't he calling her? She set the phone in her lap, resisting the strong urge to call him. She was from the old school way of thinking-- it was the guy's responsibility to call the girl. She even said out loud, "I'm about to blow this relationship because I am about to call this guy, which is not my style!"

Then she prayed to God, "Lord, if this relationship is of you, then he needs to call me."

"BRRIIIINNG!" Yes, you guessed it. It was Greg calling her, immediately after she prayed that prayer! God answered with a phone call. And since that time on, Greg and Gail have shared a life together.

God's Calling - Our Blessing!

God is so good -
He gives us everything we need.
He has given us each other
And He's made us family.

He has brought us all together,
Each so different and unique,
And tells us, "Love each other
And only words uplifting speak."

He gives each of us a job to do
That helps His plan unfold;
And, in the doing, Grace abounds
And Mercy yet untold.

As God put His plan in motion
To utilize His sheep,
He knew they would need a shepherd
To guide, direct, and keep.

So He looked them over one by one
And called them out by name.
They were to be God's anointed,
And they would never be the same!

The task is tough - uphill both ways -
Not for the weak of heart!
It's a special man that God does call,
His power to impart.

He must be strong yet gentle,
Very wise, yet ever learning.
He must be bold and daring,
Yet patient, praying, yearning!

The sheep are all so different,
There's not one that is the same.
It keeps a Pastor on his toes,
As "Unity" he proclaims!

But the task is not impossible,
So don't give up, my friend.
God has a miracle on the way -
And it's just around the bend!

And to our Pastors here today,
Your sheep want you to know,
We're so glad that God has placed you here
To oversee *His River Flow!!*

Jill Kidd

-84-

"Pay close attention to what you hear. The closer you listen, the more understanding you will be given - and you will receive even more."

Mark 4:24 (NLT)

Long Life?
by Holly

Living with cystic fibrosis was a difficult struggle for my son, Benny. He spent almost as much time in the hospital as he spent out. He had endured many lung infections and bowel blockages. By the time he was 19, the doctors had told him he needed to be on oxygen 24/7. He had only 18% lung capacity and about two years to live.

Of course, there was the other option of having a double lung transplant. But the stories he had been told about lung transplants only added more doom and gloom. "Half the patients die within the first year;" "So and so had a transplant and died two years later from not taking their meds properly;" and "There are no statistics on increasing life expectancy; it just may increase your quality of life." These kind of statements didn't give him (or me) much hope!

One day, I took Benny to a routine doctor's appointment at Loma Linda Hospital. He was supposed to be using his oxygen at all times now, but he refused. He didn't want to look like a little old man carrying around oxygen! He was still only a teenager! But when the nurse came in, she scolded him: "You know you need to be wearing your oxygen! You'll never get on the transplant list unless you start complying with doctor's orders!"

Of course the nurse meant well. She had known Benny since he was a little kid. She also knew that he was slowly dying . . . and she was concerned. But her comment really upset Benny. His life seemed hopeless. He was slowly losing all his lung capacity and there didn't seem to be much hope in receiving a lung transplant. He punched the wall and hollered out in anger and frustration.

All I could do was watch the whole scenario unfold. What could I say? I had no answers or words of comfort. My son was dying and there was nothing I could do about it. It was times like these, though, that the words of the prophecy I received when I was pregnant with him sustained me. "Your baby is going to be alright." I was "hard pressed, but not crushed; perplexed, but not in despair."

I had faith, but what about Benny? We drove home in silence. He was angry and frustrated and I didn't know what to say. I dropped him off at the house, then drove to a friend's house. I knew she was a prayer warrior, and I was really in need of prayer right then. We prayed together, then I went home and opened up my Bible.

God often speaks to me through his Word, and this was one of those very distinct times. I turned to Psalm 91. When I read the last three verses, my heart skipped a beat. I knew this was God talking to me about my son, Benny.

"Because he loves Me," says the Lord, "I will rescue him;
I will protect him, for he acknowledges My name.
He will call on Me, and I will answer him;
I will be with him in trouble, I will deliver him and honor him.
With long life I will satisfy him and show him My salvation."
Psalm 91:14-16

I was excited! I didn't know how it could possibly be true. "With long life I will satisfy him?" How could that be? They just gave him two years to live, and he's only 19! I quickly called him to my room.

"Benny, you have to listen to this!" I read him the scripture. It had the exact same effect on him as it did on me! He totally received it as a word from the Lord. In fact, he says that's the first time he's ever heard God speak to him! His whole countenance changed and he was filled with hope.

Three years later, Benny received a double lung transplant. He said it was the most painful thing he's ever gone through, but it transformed his life. No more oxygen, no more breathing treatments, no more running out of breath after a few steps; now he can walk and run and ride a skateboard and . . . breathe!

And if you look on his leg, you'll see a tattoo of God's hands holding a pair of lungs with the inscription, "Psalm 91:14-16."

Love Is a Powerful Weapon

Inspiration received by Holly Placencia

Follow My example. Treat people the way I treat them. You cannot please everybody. You will at times be persecuted for doing what's right. Continue to do what's right. Continue to please Me in your actions. Don't lash back when someone lashes out at you. Don't attack when you're being attacked. You can't put out fire with fire. Remember, a soft answer turns away wrath. Just speak the truth, then drop it. Let Me take care of the rest.

Obey Me without fear. What others do or say or how they feel is not your responsibility. I require you to obey Me. My love looks past what people say or how they think.

It's true, you are in a battle, a spiritual battle. The weapon I have given you to fight with is love. Love is more powerful than hate or anger or fear. You want to fight back with convincing words, but that will get you nowhere. It's a spiritual battle. You can't fight a spiritual battle with logic or common sense. When the spiritual attack comes, pray. But continue to pray throughout the entire attack. Don't stop and start using logic! Pray through. Allow my spirit to do a work. Satan is your enemy. He wars against your soul. Don't give in. Keep praying and keep fighting. Use the weapons I have given you. Speak the Word of God. Let the Word of God fill your mind and your soul.

*"Listen and pay attention!
Do not be arrogant,
for the Lord has spoken."*

Jeremiah 13:15 (NLT)

Rapture Vision
by Jill

It was a weeknight and 20 or so people were gathered at church for our scheduled Berean Study Group. I had been wanting classes like these for years, and finally I found them. Since others were interested, we formed a study group that met weekly. I was so excited about these classes, I took many of them on my own as well as joining the class for the current study. Our pastor taught them initially and then invited me to teach some of them as well. A challenge and a joy!

On this particular night, the pastor was teaching. I was in the sound room working the PowerPoint slides for the pastor. There were 6 long tables set up, 3 on each side of the area we were using. Everyone sat on one side of the table, facing the teacher and projection screen. The sound room was in the back.

Class was underway, and I was being attentive to keep up with the slides as the pastor directed me. Then suddenly, it became deathly quiet! The pastor was not talking – in fact, he was not there! I saw the four people at the table in front of me begin to rise – actually they were lifted up from their seated position – all at the same time. And then they were gone! As I stared into the room, as if through a window in time, the stark quietness was eerie. Most of the room had been emptied. But there were a few individuals scattered in the room that were now standing and looking all around, obviously bewildered and perplexed. The Lord didn't show me their faces, as the room seemed very distant now. Then – everyone was back, the pastor was teaching as if nothing had happened, and I tried to catch up with the PowerPoint slides. Next thing I knew, the vision repeated itself! Exactly the same! Strangely quiet, watching the same four rise from their chairs, no sound coming from the pastor teaching in the front. Gone – most of them! Those who were left behind, looking around, bewildered – quiet – eerie! No one moved except for looking around.

I realized the Lord had shown me a vision of what it would be like if He returned that night. Seeing the same thing twice seemed to validate it even more for me. I kept it to myself several days, but could not shake it from my memory or my spirit. Finally, I shared it with the pastor. I also shared with him that I felt compelled to tell the class what I had seen. There was a warning there – to Bible students! – that not everyone was ready. Some, right in that study group, would be left behind if they weren't warned – if they didn't make things right with the Lord!

The next time we met, I stood before the class and recounted what I had been shown - not once, but twice! It was very sobering for all of us. After class, two people came, at different times, and asked me if it was them that was left behind. I explained that the Lord did not reveal to me any faces (thankfully).

I am sure the Holy Spirit was working to redeem any that paid attention to this warning. No one dropped out of the classes at that time, and we continued growing together in the Lord!

His Power He's Revealed

They say, "Seeing is believing," but in Christ it is not so.
First, we must believe, and then we see.
For then, and only then, can His glory be revealed
And newness come alive in you and me!

We've heard, "Faith can move the mountains," but this faith I've little of,
So I praise the Lord my frailties He knows.
The seed of the mustard is the tiniest of all,
But with that tiny bit of faith His glory glows!

His "Saving Grace" is perfect, but His "Healing Grace" is more -
It's His promise of abundant life today.
The world He wants to give us - Open wide the Glory Doors!
We mean more to Him than words could ever say!

Raise your hands to the Heavens and know that God is God!
Surrender all to the One who saved your soul;
For He, and He alone, can lead you safely home,
And only He can truly make you whole!

He is greater than the greatest! His power He's revealed!
He is King of kings and Lord of all the lords!
He heals us in an instant; mends our hearts and binds our souls,
And He keeps us to Himself for evermore!

King of kings and Lord of lords;
Great Physician; Holy One;
Prince of Peace; Holy Spirit;
God the Father; God the Son!

Jill Kidd

"Anyone with ears to hear must listen to the Spirit and understand what He is saying to the churches. To everyone who is victorious I will give some of the manna that has been hidden away in heaven. And I will give to each one a white stone, and on the stone will be engraved a new name that no one understands except the one who receives it."

Revelation 2:17 (NLT)

The Battle Belongs to the Lord
by Holly

God speaks to His children in so many different ways. He spoke to me by a prophetic utterance from an evangelist. He has spoken to Jill many times through poetry. Neva saw a vision. He spoke to Benny and to many of us through the Word of God. Sandra felt God speak to her entire being. Shirley heard the audible voice of God.

So what's Gail's story? How did God speak to her? We laughed when we heard this one!

She was in the car one day with her little 4-year-old daughter strapped in the carseat in the back. At the time, Gail was very upset about something (she doesn't even remember now what the problem was). Talking out loud, she was painting a picture of an impossible situation. She was frustrated, had no answers, and felt completely hopeless about the particular problem she was facing. But as she went on and on about it, a little voice piped up from the backseat and said,

"Mom! Did you forget that ***the battle belongs to the Lord?***"

Yes, this word from God came straight from the mouth of a preschooler! This little girl had been in Sunday School learning all about the story of David and Goliath. It's no wonder Gail can't even remember what the problem was that she had been so worked up about at the time! When she heard those words, she was stopped in her tracks. These were words from scripture!

And these words have come back to her so many times since then. When she faces seemingly impossible situations, feeling frustrated or depressed, Gail remembers that ***"the battle belongs to the Lord."***

I Will Lead You Through the Pain

Inspiration received by Holly Placencia

Draw near to Me and I will draw near to you. I have plans for you. Just wait on Me. Follow Me and keep Me your main focus. I am leading you. Don't stress over things. Trust Me and lean on Me. I am leading you. You have to go through disappointments sometimes. Everybody has disappointments. Just feel the pain of the disappointment and I will lead you through it. I don't lead you around it to avoid it. I lead you through it. Disappointments are painful but you have to walk through it. You won't grow by avoiding it or masking over it. You had high hopes, but they were crushed. You believed something so strongly, but now that belief is shaken. Walk with Me through the disappointment. I will bring you through it. I will not let you down. I will strengthen you through it. It's okay to feel hurt and sad. It won't last forever.

"Today when you hear
His voice,
don't harden your hearts .. .

Hebrews 3:7 (NLT)

Dial: P-R-A-Y-E-R
by Holly

Shirley's son, Randy, was born with asthma. By the time he was just two years old, he had it really bad. He had to take several medications per day and use the breathing machine regularly. His frequent wheezing was a constant concern to Shirley.

One day, while she was washing the breakfast dishes, Randy was sitting in front of the TV watching Sesame Street. She noticed he was wheezing but it didn't seem that bad at the time. But as she was watching him, he suddenly fell over sideways! He actually stopped breathing for a moment, until the wheezing started again.

Shirley quickly loaded Randy up in the car along with Brian, his younger brother, and rushed to the doctor. She called her mom to meet her there so she could help her with the baby. They arrived at the doctor's at about 9:15 a.m. and stayed throughout the day. The whole time, Randy kept wheezing and wheezing. They gave him four different breathing treatments and at least two or three steroid shots. By about noon, he was throwing up mucus balls that looked kind of like fuzz balls. He was throwing up so much that he started coughing up blood. Around 4:30, the doctor said that by all rights he should admit him into the hospital. He didn't want to do that, though, because he knew that hospital procedure in those days was to make him sleep under a tent. That would stress the poor little guy out even more, and probably make his breathing even worse. He suggested that Shirley take him home and just watch him carefully. They had already given him all the medicine that they could and it didn't appear to have any effect on him. Who knows, maybe it would kick in later. Little Randy continued wheezing and struggling with every breath, and the doctor didn't know what else to do about it.

So Shirley took him home. She sat her little boy down on the couch and went to get him some apple juice. That's when she heard the audible voice of the Lord speak to her, as clear as day:

**"If you had called the prayer chain,
you wouldn't have had to go through all this!"**

"Oh, Lord, you are so right," Shirley responded. She picked up the phone and called the prayer chain at church. They started praying, Randy started breathing, and the asthma attack was completely gone!

Darkest Before Dawn

When you're standing on the promises
That God so clearly gave,
And suddenly you feel you've been knocked down;
And the darkness is so deep
That you can't see the light of day,
Just press on, ye saints, press on!

For when the darkness deepens,
You can only walk by faith;
So pick up your shield and fight the fight head on.
For the break of light is coming,
When the victory you'll see.
So press on, ye saints, press on!

For the Lord just wants to strengthen
And equip you for His use.
Your trust in Him He only wants to build.
And in His gentle mercy
He'll uphold you with His hand.
So press on, ye saints, press on!

So rejoice! And know, in times like these,
That, just around the bend,
The promise of the Lord you'll surely see!
If only you'll remember
It's the darkest before dawn,
And press on, ye saints, press on!!

Jill Kidd

"Anyone with ears to hear
must listen to the Spirit
and understand what He is
saying to the churches.
To everyone who is victorious
I will give fruit
from the tree of life
in the paradise of God."

Revelation 2:7 (NLT)

Gas for God's Girls
by Holly

Sometimes when God answers prayer, He doesn't say anything. He just points us in the right direction. And sometimes He performs a miracle provision that leaves us standing there with our jaws dropped all the way down to our chins in absolute awe of how great our God is!

This is what happened to sisters, Carrie and Shirley, as they were travelling from California to Kentucky. They had been driving a long time through the deserts of Arizona and New Mexico. There was nothing around them for miles and miles-- no houses, no people, no towns, not even any road signs. They felt like they were out in the middle of nowhere. It was getting late at night and they were running out of gas. In fact, they were completely on empty! Not knowing what else to do, they just kept on going, and they prayed hard!

Soon they saw a sign that said, "Food, Gas, Lodging." Thank God! He heard their prayer and was pointing them in the right direction! So they pulled off the road, went over the bridge, and around the side of the mountain. There they saw a nice little lake with a boat docked and a small cafe. There were lights on in the cafe with a couple of people inside. And to their great relief, there was a single gas pump outside. Nobody was around, but they were able to use their card and fill up their tank with gas.

But this isn't the end of the story! Carrie and Shirley spent a week in Kentucky and now were on their way back to California. As they were driving through those long stretches of desert again, they wanted to go back to the same place where they had stopped for gas before. Soon they found a sign that said "Food, Gas, Lodging" and they knew it was the same place. Once again, they pulled off the road, went over the bridge and around the mountain.

But what they saw this time is what left them standing with mouths wide open and in complete amazement of an awesome God who cares deeply for His children! There was no lake and no boat. There was an old, deserted building that obviously hadn't been used for many years. And there was no gas pump at all!

God answered the desperate cries of Carrie and Shirley by not only pointing them in the right direction, but also by performing an outright miracle!

Give God the Glory

Inspiration received by Holly Placencia

Go...you need to speak. I will give you words. Just ask Me when you don't know what to say. Don't think of yourself, think of the other person. I've given you a mission field. This mission field is for you to go out and reach them; it's not to flaunt yourself. Don't hold back. Let My love shine through you. Allow Me to speak through you. Allow Me to love through you. I want the glory. I want people to look to Me. I'm the one who can help them, not you. That's why you need to direct them to Me. Don't worry about what other people think of you. Some will like you and some won't. If you're worried about what they think of you, then the focus is you. Let Me be your focus.

"*Listen, you women,
to the words of the Lord;
open your ears to what
He has to say.*"

Jeremiah 9:20 (NLT)

Now What!?
by Jill

I received the phone call the afternoon of my 63rd birthday. We were celebrating at my daughter's home. My daughter and her mother-in-law were with me in the living room when my cell phone rang. It was my doctor. They watched me as I listened intently to the results of the biopsy. I couldn't stop the tears from running down my cheeks as I continued listening. Their faces reflected that the news I was receiving was not what we had been hoping for. It was confirmed - I had breast cancer. The good news was it was caught early. I would need surgery and radiation, but not chemo. But on my birthday!? Happy birthday to me...

It took a day or two, or maybe three, before I actually realized that it *was* a great birthday gift after all. If it had not been discovered it would not have been treated. Untreated, who knows how many more birthdays I would have had. Yes, indeed, happy birthday to me, after all!!!

The surgery went very well and, after 23 radiation treatments, I was doing great! I was prescribed a medication that helps prevent breast cancer from returning, and the future looked bright and cheery. Until . . .

Now what? What was attacking my body!? I could barely move! I walked by taking tiny little baby steps. And even *that* took a lot of effort. I could hardly move my shoulders and arms. It seemed like all the muscles in my body were seizing up. First cancer, now this! Whatever it was!

My younger sister, Joyce, decided I needed a get-away time and whisked me down to her timeshare in Palm Springs. How lovely! Whenever we're together we have a Scrabble marathon, and this time was no different. But, it *was* Palm Springs, and there *was* a pool, so we would go out for a dip whenever we wanted. But, as I shuffled along, taking my little baby steps, it was just too painful to make the effort.

Our second night there, as we both were getting more and more worried about me, I had a vision in the wee hours of the morning. I had never experienced anything quite like that before or since. Suddenly, I saw myself sitting in a chair in my new oncologist's office. My daughter was in the chair next to me, and we were listening to the doctor explain what was going to happen over the next several months of my treatment. It was like a tape being played of my first visit with the oncologist. Everything was crystal clear and I heard him speaking to us exactly as he did during that first visit five months earlier. He laid out the plan. First, the surgery, then radiation. Then I would be prescribed medication to prevent recurrence. Next, he began to explain some of the side effects of the medication. Among the side effects, he mentioned muscles seizing up. Oh my goodness! There it was! That's what was going on with me. I don't know why I never thought about side effects! I was doing so well. I just thought something *else* had come upon me.

I believe the Lord gave me that vision – an exact replica of my experience in the doctor's office months earlier – so I could hear, again, what I had forgotten about. As soon as they opened, I called my oncologist to report my symptoms and was told to stop the medication immediately. Well, of course, I already had! It took about a year to get full range of motion again, but I did get it back.

The Lord gave me a second look at the day I first met my oncologist so I could hear, again, what had been forgotten. He is so amazing! And I am so thankful!

He Loves Even Me!

He loves me! He loves me!
He told me so today.
I asked Him, "Are you with me, Lord?"
And He answered right away:
"I will never leave you
Or forsake you."
And I knew at once -
It's true!
He loves me! He loves me!
He loves even me!

He loves me! He loves me!
There's nothing more to say!
I felt His arm around me
As He guided me today.
I heard Him gently laughing
When I questioned was He there.
And He drew me close and held me
In my moment of despair.
He loves me! He loves me!
He loves even me!

Jill Kidd

"Listen to Me,

you who know

right from wrong,

you who cherish My

law in your hearts. . ."

Isaiah 51:7 (NLT)

Leaning on the Motorcycle
by Holly

My parents had spent the last 10 years as missionaries, first in Ecuador, then in Papua New Guinea. My dad was an experienced pilot, flying much needed people and supplies into the remote villages. This enabled the linguists to continue their work of translating the Bible into many different languages. And my mom, well . . . she took care of us 5 children.

When my older sister was ready to graduate from high school, my youngest sister was just two years old. My parents knew their time of being missionaries was coming to an end. They needed to return to the United States and help their older children get settled in their lives. My mom was looking forward to moving back to Ohio where they were both from, and where her parents lived. She hadn't spent much time with her mother over the past 10 years; now she was imagining all the time they would spend together . . . the conversations, the shopping, the cooking, the catching up. Okay, maybe there was the guilt complex that played a part as well. Her mother was getting older and was suffering from rheumatoid arthritis. She wanted to be there to help take care of her.

There was also the possibility of the family moving to North Carolina. My dad's mom lived there, as well as other family members. My parents also owned some property there. My uncle was a builder; he could build us a house on that property. My mom really preferred moving to Ohio to be close to her mom, but the idea of North Carolina seemed doable. They would be living near family and friends, and she could make several trips a year to go visit my grandparents in Ohio. As my mom contemplated these possibilities of where to live, she became quite comfortable with either plan. She had enjoyed her time on the mission field; she knew God had called them to serve in other countries. But now she was looking forward to living close to family once again.

But wait a minute! There was a huge problem! My dad wasn't thinking along these lines in the least bit. He approached my mom one day, happy and excited about his new idea.

"Honey, I want to start an airline. I want to make it a Christian airline and use it as a way to spread the Gospel. We could play Christian music and give reduced prices to missionaries."

"An airline?" my mom questioned.

"Yes," my dad exclaimed excitedly. He had the plan all figured out in his mind. He told my mom he planned to sell their property in North Carolina so he would have the money to start this airline. He was excited and ready to start a new adventure. In my mom's mind, she ruled out the possibility of living in North Carolina, since he was planning on selling the property. That means they could live in Ohio near her mother, while my dad tried out this hairbrain idea!

But then my dad went on... "Of course, we would have to live in a place that's practical for running an airline. I've got that all figured out too . . . California!"

My mom nearly fell off her seat. California? CALIFORNIA? That's hundreds of miles away from her mother! And isn't that the place where the most ungodly people lived? It would be a horrible place to raise their children! They had never been there, they had no friends there and no relatives. How did he come up with such a crazy idea? It was time to put her foot down. Absolutely not! There was no way she was moving to California!

Later that day, my mom sat in her chair, possibly dozing off a little. She had a dream... or was she daydreaming? Or maybe it was a vision . . . she doesn't really know. But one thing was for sure-- she knew this "dream" was from God. She saw herself riding on the back of a motorcycle with her husband as the driver. This was a common occurrence there in New Guinea since a motorcycle was our only means of transportation. My dad had taught her how to lean with him to the right when they turned right or to the left when they turned left. This would prevent him from losing control of the motorcycle.

So this dream (or vision) was nothing out of the ordinary . . . until she no longer saw herself on the back of the motorcycle. Suddenly, she was up on top of his shoulders! And she was not the type of woman who enjoyed getting a thrill from risky behavior! But that's when she distinctly heard the Lord tell her:

"Lean with your husband."

As long as she leaned with her husband, she was safe up there on his shoulders.

Soon after that, we all left Papua New Guinea and returned to the United States. With a determination in my dad's mind to try something new and different, and a simple trust in my mom's heart that she was being obedient to God, the family moved to California.

What happened to the airline business? It never flew. What happened to the money from the property? Gone. What about us kids? We all settled in California, had kids of our own, and are starting to have grandkids. Our roots are in California and it's where we all call home. Where is my mom's mother now? In heaven with Jesus.

My mom wonders at times what would have happened if she hadn't listened to God and insisted on doing what she wanted. It would have either split up the family or caused a lot of strife and resentment. Was my dad's idea of a Christian airline from God? Nobody really knows. But one thing my mom is confident about . . . God told her to follow her husband. That's what she did, and they are a happily married couple to this day, surrounded by many children, grandchildren, and great-grandchildren!

I Hear Your Prayers

Inspiration received by Holly Placencia

I hear your prayers and I am answering them. Things go on in the spirit realm that you can't see. Keep praying and don't give up. You will learn a lot through prayer, and you will grow a lot. Prayer brings peace. Don't be discouraged about your job situation. I know what I'm doing. I work behind the scenes in the spirit realm. You need to trust Me in this matter. I will give you what's best for you. Think of Me as your employer. I do the hiring and the firing. You are working for Me. You are working on My pay scale. The amazing thing is, I'm the Employer who knows exactly what's best for you! I know you inside and out. I know the right job, the right pay, and the right location. You can trust Me.

Then Jesus called to the
crowd to come and hear.
"All of you listen,"
He said, "and try to understand."

Mark 7:14 (NLT)

God's Divine Appointment
by Holly

Gail was a little nervous as she anticipated her dad coming for a visit. She loved her dad, but she had never had a very close relationship with him. Her parents were divorced and he had remarried. Since he spent most of his time with his wife, it was rare for Gail to have any one-on-one time with her dad.

Now Gail was happily married with two young children, and Dad and his wife were coming to visit. There were a number of things going through her mind concerning this visit, but when she woke up that morning, only one thing rang loud and clear to her inner spirit. She knew it was the Lord speaking:

> *"Gail, you have a divine appointment*
> *with your dad today. Be ready!"*

And from that moment on, a series of events took place that were entirely orchestrated by God. She didn't know what was going to happen or what she was to say, but God took her through it step by step.

Soon after her dad and stepmom arrived, Gail said to him, "Dad, can we go take a drive?" She wanted some alone time with her dad, which was something that rarely happened. To her surprise, her dad answered, "Sure," then he told his wife that he was going for a drive and would be back soon. Also to her surprise, and relief, her stepmom was perfectly fine with it.

When they got in the car, the Lord impressed upon Gail to let her dad know what was going on. So she said, "Dad, the Lord has a divine appointment for you today." Her dad had been raised in a Christian home but had steered far from it. He had his own way of thinking and his own way of believing. So he raised his eyebrows and said, "Oh really?"

Now Gail almost felt like she was in a dream! Things seemed to be falling into place perfectly and she hadn't even planned it in advance! As they started driving, the Lord impressed upon her to go to Lenhester Park, which was a park nearby that held a lot of meaning to Gail and her husband, Greg.

As they drove up to the park, Gail started telling her dad why this park had so much meaning to them. She said, "Dad, this park is very special to me and Greg, and I'm going to tell you why. Several years ago when we were first married, Greg and I lost our first child. This is the park we came to, to give that child back to the Lord. It was a very difficult time for us."

With tears in his eyes, Gail's dad took her hand and said, "I didn't know; I'm so sorry."

"I know; I never told you," Gail responded. "But when I woke up this morning, God told me that I have a divine appointment with you today. I realized as we were driving over here that I am meant to tell you this story. We were devastated to the very core when we lost that child. We felt like we had done everything right-- we served God in ministry, we were virgins when we got married, we did the whole marriage thing the right way--- Why God? Why would you take our first child?"

Gail continued to look at her dad and speak with a heart full of passion. "Dad, I think I know now part of God's purpose in taking that child. When I get to heaven, I'm going to find that baby, and I'm going to hold that baby for about a thousand years. But when I put that baby down, the very next person I want to see there . . . is you. But I don't know that I will."

"Well, uh," her dad started to speak, but Gail continued.

"Do you have things right between you and God?" Gail became very honest with him. "Is Christ the Lord of your life?"

"Oh Honey, I've done all that," her dad responded, with an "I know more than you" kind of attitude.

But Gail continued on. "It's the desire of my heart to see you there. I know our story hasn't been the greatest story, but someday we can have a better story. I just want to be sure I'm going to see you there. Can we pray together?"

To Gail's absolute joy and amazement, her dad answered, "Sure, we can do that." Right then and there, Gail led her dad in the sinner's prayer, and he dedicated his life to the Lord.

After the prayer, they drove back to the house. What seemed like hours had only been about 15 minutes! But God's divine appointment had been accomplished, and Gail now has the assurance that she will see her dad one day in heaven. Praise the Lord!

Hallelujah, I'm Born Again!

Praise the Lord on High for He gave to me
A gift far richer than gold.
I was trapped inside a hopeless shell
'Til my Jesus made me whole.

The enemy had robbed me;
Stripped me of all worth;
Hooked me with the things of Earth
Baited with *some* Truth.

But Jesus kept on calling
Until finally I did hear.
"They're lies," He said, "Deny him.
Follow Me, and do not fear."

He led me to the high road
That, before, I never saw.
He took my hand and held on tight,
And He healed my wounds, so raw.

Hallelujah, I'm born again!
Jesus Christ has set me free!
He shed His light on the evil one
And enabled me to see.

Jill Kidd

"... Let all My words sink deep into your own heart first. Listen to them carefully for yourself."

Ezekiel 3:10 (NLT)

Do What's Right
by Holly

Sheila had a very abusive father while she was growing up. He was an alcoholic. And he was mean ... physically, verbally, and emotionally. As she and her older sister entered their teen years, the abuse became worse and worse. A lot of it was directed toward their mother, and the two girls and younger brother often had to step in to protect their mom. Sheila was terrified of her dad and hated him for the pain he caused her and her family.

Finally, when she was 14 years old, Sheila's mom announced that she would be getting a divorce. Sheila said that was the happiest day of her life! What a relief to be away from that situation! She no longer had to be around the anger, the belittling, the insults, the shame, and the physical abuse. In fact, her mom eventually married again, this time to a wonderful man. Sheila loved her new dad. He was the one she would look up to and interact with and consider her real dad for the rest of his time on this earth.

So what happened to the first dad, the one who was her father by blood? After the divorce, she saw him occasionally, but those times became fewer and farther apart. She was hurt and angry about how he had treated her and how he had treated her mother. And he seemed to show no remorse. Finally, she had had enough. Sheila made a decision to completely cut him out of her life. She wanted nothing more to do with him! Even though her older sister (who has a big heart) would continue to interact with him occasionally, Sheila never saw him or spoke to him for over 10 years.

During this time, though, God was continually tugging at her heart. She knew about God from her grandparents. They would take her to church whenever she went to visit. But she basically lived her life doing what she wanted. She married, had a son, and eventually divorced.

As she entered her 40's, she fell in love with a Christian man named Bill. They attended church together regularly, and Sheila committed her life to the Lord. The two had been living together for some time, but God convicted them about that, so they decided the right thing to do would be to get married.

Sheila's walk with God became stronger and stronger as the years went by. She noticed how God had always been by her side, nudging and pulling her to the way that was good and right. He also started planting thoughts in her head concerning her dad. But these thoughts were not the angry, bitter thoughts that she had always had in the past. God was beginning to soften her heart toward him.

One day Sheila had an encounter with the Lord. She doesn't remember the exact words that God said, but she remembers the experience and the message very well.

"You can't change your father, but it's your responsibility to do the right thing regardless of what he does or doesn't do."

At that moment, Sheila knew she had to get things right with her dad. She knew she had to forgive him in her heart. She knew she had to reach out to him and be the daughter that God meant for her to be, no matter how he responded. When she made up her mind to do this, a peace came all over her. All those ugly feelings melted away.

The first thing she did was start sending him cards and presents for special occasions. Then she mustered up the courage to go visit him. It wasn't easy, and she didn't know what she was going to say to him. And she didn't know how he would respond. But she did it just because it was the right thing to do.

Had her dad changed over all those years? Not really. He had mellowed out a little as he grew older, but he still had his same old temper and mocking ways about him. He had no idea what he ever did to her to keep her away for all those years. But Sheila knew this was not about him, it was about her. It was about her being obedient to God and doing the right thing. She made it a point to let him know that she cared about him, and his reaction just rolled off her back like water on a duck.

A year after Sheila reunited with her dad, he passed away unexpectedly. How glad she was that she had taken the time to show him the love of God before he died. She had a peace in her heart that she had done the right thing.

Do My Will

Inspiration received by Holly Placencia

You can have joy in spite of what anyone else says or thinks. Your relationship is with Me. I am your number one. Nobody else can rule you. They only tear you down if you let them. People can have their opinions and say what they want. My requirement of you is that you serve Me, that you honor Me above all others, that you do My will. You know what My will is. I have told you. It's that you do right, that you show mercy to others, that you walk with Me. Even if no one else is following Me, you follow Me. Don't follow the world; follow Me. I am holding your hand.

"But you, son of man,
listen to what I say to you.
Do not rebel
like that rebellious people . . ."

Ezekiel 2:8 (NIV)

Victor's Victory
by Holly

Victor grew up as a pastor's kid and the son of an air force chaplain. He was well-acquainted with church work and ministry. He saw it all-- the good, the bad, and the ugly. And his life consisted of moving-- and moving and moving! Rarely did his family stay in one place more than a year. In fact, he attended 16 different schools during his growing up years!

All this moving deeply affected Victor. He lived in a very stressful, tense, and insecure environment. He found it hard to build up lasting friendships with people. Of course, there was the positive side to this, too. He learned that he could easily jump into new situations, see a need and fulfill it. It created much diversity in his life. But the instability of his home life and his longing for relationships produced an emptiness inside that was begging to be filled. That's when he turned to the thing he thought could fulfill him-- drugs and alcohol. At first it gave him a sense of freedom and it seemed like a quick fix to his problems, but soon it became a full-on addiction that he struggled with for many years.

This addiction was in stark contrast to the person that Victor truly desired to be. He recounted as a child being at a church service sitting next to his mom. He watched her as she sang and worshiped the Lord with her hands raised high. He felt the presence of God! How he longed for that in his own life! He cried out to God and received Jesus Christ as his own personal Savior. A heart of worship was born.

This began a long battle in his life of wanting to please the Lord but yet struggling with substance abuse. Many times he cried out to God to help him, and many times he fell back into his addiction. He was like the Apostle Paul who said, *"Although I want to do good, evil is right there with me. For in my inner being I delight in God's law, but I see another law at work in me, waging war against the law of my mind and making me a prisoner of the law of sin at work within me. What a wretched man I am! Who will rescue me from this body that is subject to death?"* (Romans 7:22-24)

Victor found out, just as the Apostle Paul did, that the answer was found in Jesus Christ. It meant dying to himself and allowing Christ to reign in his life. But that doesn't come easy, and there was still a long road ahead of him.

Let's fast-forward to the year 2016. Victor was now in his late 40's and owned his own business. But his mother became very sick and was dying. He was very distraught about this and wanted to be there for her during her last days. But as he spent time with his mom, he wasn't able to hold the business together. Sadly, his mom passed away, he lost his business, and he soon found himself homeless and living in a men's shelter. Depression and anxiety began to overtake him.

He had spent nearly 90 days in the shelter and he knew his time was almost up. He sat quiet before God, not knowing what to do or where to go next. That's when God spoke to his heart. He said,

"I am bringing you to the end of yourself."

When Victor told me that, I asked him, "So God brought you to the end of yourself and that's when you put Him on the throne and made Him Lord of your life?"

"No, no, you don't understand," he hastened to tell me, "it's a process. He said he is *BRINGING* me to the end of myself. I'm still living out what that means."

I thought to myself, "Of course. Have any of us actually come to the end of ourselves this side of heaven?"

When God spoke to Victor, he was encouraged. He realized that he could no longer be motivated by selfish gain. It had to be intentional surrender to God on a daily basis. Eventually the depression and anxiety he had been experiencing began to be lifted. He was able to move out of the shelter and find employment. He entered a line of work which requires helping others, which brings him much fulfillment. Now he lives in San Bernardino, California, and cares for his young son. He's teaching his son to pray every day and worship God, just as he saw his own mother doing. There's a smile on Victor's face and a joy in his heart as he has learned the secret of living . . . less of self and more of God!

The Master Mechanic

I was just an old jalopy traveling down the road,
My color barely peeking through my heavy, awkward load.
My tires were worn and wobbly - barely hanging on!
And my windshield was so dirty it was hard to see the sun.

My horn was loud and brassy, if it even worked at all!
And my seats were covered over to hide the rips and soil.
I used to hold a lot of friends as we went running here and there,
But now no one comes near me, they don't love me - they don't care.

I was headed for a breakdown and, having no where else to go,
I headed for the old garage and a Mechanic I didn't know.
But He was gentle and understanding and invited me to stay.
So I decided I would trust Him - I was out of gas, anyway!

He took His time as He worked with me. There wasn't any rush.
He washed (by hand) with a gentle touch and didn't scrape or brush!
He repaired the dents and dings that I had received along the way,
And even replaced the broken parts I had tried to hide away.

While I was mending, healing, waiting, He gave me many tips -
Like how to read the road maps and how to navigate the dips!
He handed me a Manual which He said I needed now;
It would keep me up and running and would even tell me how!

It was important, the Mechanic said, to keep in touch with Him,
And He handed me His business card and, with a great big grin,
He opened up the door for me and started up my engine.
He said, "It's time to go, my friend, but don't forget your lesson!"

It felt so good just being there with my new Mechanic friend,
I didn't really want to leave for I feared it all would end.
I didn't know I was forever changed and I didn't need to panic.
It took some time to understand that my Friend is the **Master Mechanic!**

I'm still an old jalopy, but I'm running on New Gas!
My color's bright and shiny and my load is light at last!
My tires are running smoothly and I even have a spare;
My windshield wipers work so well that, when it rains, I don't care!

Now I use my gentle horn to softly summon friends,
Or to warn the weary traveler of a danger or dead-end.
With all the trash and junk thrown out, my seats accommodate
All my friends, both old and new, come early or come late!

The road's the same, but now I've learned, through my Mechanic Friend,
New tips on navigation until my journey's end.
I gave it up and trusted Him, but He has given it back to me -
He cleaned and fixed and made me new - **The Master Mechanic Set Me Free!**

Jill Kidd

But even as he spoke,
a bright cloud overshadowed them,
and a voice from the cloud said,
"This is my dearly loved Son,
who brings Me great joy.
Listen to Him."

Matthew 17:5 (NLT)

God's Messenger
by Holly

Three years after my son, Benny, had his double lung transplant, he was feeling pretty good. He could do things that he was never able to do before. He could walk places, ride a skateboard, enjoy the beach, hang out with friends, just breathe! He tells people that he accepted Jesus as his Savior when he was 18, but he truly made Him the Lord of his life after his lung transplant at 22 years old. He was so grateful to be alive! He decided he wanted to go to Bible college.

This was a brand new venture for him. In late August 2013, Benny started Calvary Chapel Bible College in Murrieta, California, along with his younger brother, David. They were happy to be in college together and Benny was excited about his future.

There was one small problem, though. Even though his lung capacity had improved 100% from receiving a new pair of lungs, he still struggled with digestion problems, as is usually the case with anyone with cystic fibrosis. Many times throughout his life he had to be hospitalized for stomach blockages. He had surgery at birth and again at three years old. Now he was 25 and the stomach blockages seemed to be increasing. These were minor inconveniences to Benny who was used to spending time in the hospital. But it wasn't going to stop him from moving on and doing what was in his heart to do.

Three weeks after he started Bible college, he experienced a little bit of stomach pain. It was a Friday evening and he asked his brother to drive him to the hospital in San Diego. He called me on the phone and told me what they were doing. He said it was no big deal and that he should be back in school on Monday.

But, unfortunately, it was a big deal. It was something that would have a tremendous effect on him for the next two years of his life. He had a stomach blockage, and this time the doctors felt that surgery was necessary. Benny doesn't remember any of this. The surgery nearly killed him. He was in a coma for a month and kept alive on life support for two months. His lungs filled up with fluid. He developed five different lung infections, causing his lungs to shut down completely. He lost so much weight, his appearance was like a skeleton. The doctors gave him no hope of survival. By all human standards, he should have died. He was hospitalized for a total of 5 months, but in and out of the hospital almost weekly for about two years. Needless to say, he was forced to drop out of college. It was a very bleak and dark time for him, and of course, very disappointing.

By Christmas 2013, he was off life support and just starting the long, upward road to health. He was nowhere near ready to leave the hospital yet, but he was able to get out of his bed for short periods of time. Two days before Christmas, Benny was feeling exceptionally discouraged. He cried out to God, "Lord, I need a word of encouragement. Send someone to speak to me. Give me a messenger; send me an angel!"

The next day, his five brothers and I went out to the hospital to spend Christmas Eve with him. We were all sitting in the lobby playing a card game. Earlier in the day, Benny had learned something about how many gallons of water Jesus had turned into wine; some piece of Bible trivia that he thought was interesting. I don't remember exactly what he said about it, but he decided to share his knowledge with the rest of us there in the lobby.

After he said this, a young man from another part of the lobby stood up and approached our little group. He introduced himself as "Landon" and said he overheard someone talking about the Bible. He then began to tell us story after story of things he had seen God do in other people's lives. He mentioned people with lung transplants and stomach blockages and other things that Benny totally related to, all the while not knowing even one thing about Benny's condition!

The more Landon talked, the more passionate he became. We all sat there spellbound as we listened to him! He told Benny that God has a plan for his life, that God was going to heal him and deliver him. He prayed for Benny and we all felt the anointing and power of God as he prayed. We had no idea who this guy was or where he came from, but we knew he was definitely sent by God to bring a message to Benny.

It wasn't until the summer of 2015 that Benny experienced a complete recovery from that dreadful surgery in September 2013. But God did what he promised when He spoke through that young man named Landon. He healed him and delivered him from the terrible suffering he had to go through. He was able to go back to Bible college, and this time finish it.

After that encounter with Landon, Benny often wondered, "Who was that guy? Was he an angel? No, he couldn't have been." He often looked for him. Landon had said he worked at the hospital as a custodian. But Benny never saw him again . . .

Except one time. About 6 months after that encounter with him, Benny developed a serious infection and once again had to be intubated. He was placed on a gurney and wheeled into the elevator. As the elevator doors were closing, he suddenly saw Landon peek in. He looked straight at Benny, pointed his finger at him, and said, "Hang in there, Buddy."

That confirmed it in Benny's mind. Yes, Landon had to be an angel sent by God to give him a message of hope and encouragement at a time in his life when he needed it the most.

Merry Christmas!!

Jesus loves you, this I know,
Because He came to Earth to show
The way to Heaven and God, above, And
to demonstrate to you His love.

Born of a woman into the human race,
Jesus came to set the pace;
To show the way and light your path; To
ease your pain and heal your wrath.

He came in love with gentle heart;
He came with wisdom to depart.
He came to bring you peace and joy; He
came a baby, a little boy!

Rejoice! Rejoice!! The world has known
A Saviour from God's very Throne! Born
a babe; then crucified;
Jesus now stands by your side!

He's your Defender before the Throne
And He tells God you are His own! And
all you had to do was say,
"Jesus, live in my heart today."

Does Jesus love you? Yes! He does! Of
this you can be sure, because
He came from Heaven, went to the grave,
And rose again for YOU to save!

So, Merry Christmas, my dear friend,
May every sorrow, Jesus mend.
As you remember our Savior's birth,
Know: He considers YOU great worth!

Jill Kidd

"Come to Me with your ears wide open. Listen, and you will find life."

Isaiah 55:3 (NLT)

Lessons on Listening
by Jill

Helen had another story or two to tell Holly and me that overcast day in July when we met at the 7th Street Park in Yucaipa, California. After hearing her first story (Trust and Obey), we were all ears. She was such an inspiration to us and the presence of the Holy Spirit was so strong, He captured our hearts and caused us to hunger for more of Him!

First, Helen told us about this man that she did not know that was in a church service where she was. The Holy Spirit told her:

> *"That man has diabetes.*
> *You need to go and tell him that."*

She wondered, does he know it? She didn't feel confident, but she went up and told this man that she had a *hunch* (chuckling, she explained to us that she used to call it that) - She had a *hunch* that the Holy Spirit was telling her that he might have a problem with becoming diabetic. The man looked at her and said, "Is that right? I have an appointment with the doctor tomorrow."

As it turned out, he did have diabetes. Helen told him while she was talking with him to let her know, because she is also diabetic and maybe that's why the Holy Spirit was trying to connect them, because she could help him understand this disease. (Remember, too, that Helen is a nurse!)

The next week when he told her the doctor had confirmed that he did have diabetes, she thought to herself, how can I question the Holy Spirit anymore? From that point on, she no longer questioned, but trusted the Holy Spirit when He told her something. She listens carefully and discerns until she knows what He wants her to do, and then she follows His instructions. She emphasized to Holly and me that she had to learn to listen with discernment while she was listening to other people talk. She listened for the Lord to lead her. And she obeyed His instructions without questioning any longer.

We had already been there, listening intently to Helen's stories, for quite awhile. The park landscaper on a noisy lawn mower was getting closer to where we were sitting, so we leaned in to hear her better. No one wanted to leave. Perhaps it reminded her of her next *Lesson on Listening:*

Then, she continued (above the noise of the lawn mower), He sent her to Dodger Stadium. She didn't care anything about baseball, herself, but her husband did. So here she found herself, for some unknown reason, at a baseball game! According to Helen, the roaring crowd at the game was deafening, much like this guy on the lawn mower. We all laughed! But we didn't let him interfere with Helen's story. She continued: The Holy Spirit said to her in the middle of all that noise at the stadium:

"Shhh . . . listen to my voice."

So she learned that day that she could hear His still, small voice even in the roar of the crowd if she were in tune with Him, listening carefully. It doesn't have to be 100% quiet to be still before the Lord, listening. She continued, "We're in a spiritual battle and there are distractions everywhere."

Just then a siren sounded in the distance and the nerve-wracking horn of the emergency vehicle got louder as it drew closer and closer to where we were.

We weren't at a baseball game - we were at a park! There was no roar of the crowd - but there was the roar of the lawn mower coupled with the wailing of the siren. We looked at each other and nodded that we understood there were distractions all around us - and we *listened!*

My Presence Will Go With You

Inspiration received by Holly Placencia

I have commanded you to go. Now go! You will understand the language the more you are around it. Don't be intimidated or shy away from it. My presence will go with you. Stay in My presence. Let My presence guide you. I will direct you, even today. Let My presence be your guide. Just like the children of Israel followed a cloud during the day and fire at night--so I will lead you. But you won't be following Me at a distance. My presence will surround you as you go.

Constantly be aware of My presence, and listen to My instructions. You can make your plans, but ultimately I am the one leading you. I will whisper in your ear where to go, what to do, and what to say. But listen; you have to listen! Don't listen to those other voices around you. Listen to My voice. Grow accustomed to hearing My voice, then it will come to you with more and more clarity.

I will simplify your life and give you joy. Life is full of moments that can be used in obedience to Me. I won't just give you a direction for a week from now or a month from now, I will give you direction for this moment right now. Walk in My presence and you will hear My directions.

Printed in Great Britain
by Amazon

28450335R10079